LISA
霊感少女リサ
the Teenage Channeler

安河内哲也
a.k.a.
Ted Eguchi

Illustration：碧風羽

LISA
Characters

Characters 登場人物紹介

❶ ❷ ❸

③ Sara White
サラ・ホワイト

リサの母親。
不思議な能力を持つ。

① Lisa White
リサ・ホワイト

17歳の女子高生。
事故で視力を失う。

② Sister Mary
シスター・メアリー

リサの母親サラの親友。リサに
とってかけがえのない存在。

④ Dan White
ダン・ホワイト

リサの父親。

多読のすすめ

楽しめば楽しむほど、英語は読めるようになる!

　「英文多読シリーズ」は、読み出すと止まらない、ワクワクストーリーで、英語を読むことを純粋に楽しむためのものです。皆さんは、これを読み始めると、きっとストーリーの世界にハマってしまうでしょう。

　授業や参考書で精読を学び、それを繰り返し復習するのも大切な勉強です。しかし、それだけでは英文に触れる量が絶対的に不足してしまいます。ただ机で「勉強」しているだけでは、言語の修得に必要な反射神経がなかなか身に付かないのです。

　そこで、たくさんの英語に触れ、慣れるための、「多読」が必要になります。「多読」の秘訣は、勉強ではなく純粋に読書として英文を楽しむことです。

　日本語の読解も、勉強して覚えたわけではありませんよね。マンガや小説など、大好きな本を読みながら覚えたはずです。この小説は、難しい単語や構文を極力使わずに、シンプルな英語で読みやすく書かれています。でも、本当に大切な単語や熟語、構文はしっかり文の中に組み込んであります。

　「多読」のためには……
①普段勉強しているレベルより簡単であること
②内容が楽しく、興味が持てるものであること
③辞書を引いて調べることによって、読書が中断されないようにすること

　この三つが大切です。また、従来の多読教材では、「内容は簡単だけれど、語彙や表現のレベルが高すぎて読書が止まってしまう。」「内容が日本人にとっていまいち興味が持てない。」という声がよく聞かれました。

そこで、このシリーズでは以下の工夫をしました。
◎**語彙のレベルや文法のレベルを制約して、おおむね英検準2級〜センター基礎レベルの英語で、オリジナルストーリーとして書き起こした。**
◎**日本人、特に若者にとって興味が持てる内容を題材とした。イラストを随所にちりばめ読みやすくし、一度読み出すと止められなくなる工夫をした。**
◎**単語が気になる場合でも、すぐに解決できる語句注を充実させた。**
◎**朗読音声を無料でダウンロードできるようにし、耳からもストーリーが楽しめるようにした。(英語・日本語・日英対訳)**
◎**一冊分のストーリーの長さを5,000〜6,000語程度とし、ある程度読み応えはあるが、長過ぎて嫌にならないところでストーリーを完結させた。**

http://www.toshin.com/books/
※音声ダウンロードの際は、下記のパスワードが必要です。
詳細は上記のサイトをご参照ください。
Password : 2lxU4TG8
(エル)

このような学習効果を、綿密に計算して、このシリーズは作成されています。とは言っても、何より多読では、勉強のことを忘れて、純粋に楽しむことが重要です。いつでも、どこでも読んで読んで読みまくることによって、知らず知らずのうちに試験の英文も読めるようになってしまう。そんな人がたくさん生まれることを願っています。

英語だけで楽しむもよし、訳や単語・熟語の注釈を見ながら楽しむもよし、CDの朗読を聞いて楽しむのもよし。最後まで、約5,000語の冒険の旅へと出かけましょう。

安河内哲也 a.k.a. Ted Eguchi

Contents

Chapter **1** Lisa's Mission ················ 7

Chapter **2** Mother's Last message ············ 17

Chapter **3** The Voice from the Well ········ 25

Chapter **4** Time Travel ·················· 35

Chapter **5** Murderer in Disguise ············ 47

Chapter **6** Ken's Secret ·················· 61

Chapter **7** Pine Pond ···················· 75

Chapter **8** The Milky Way ·············· 85

和訳 ·· 93

索引 ·· 113

Chapter 1
Lisa's Mission

Lisa's Mission

When she was nine years old, Lisa had an accident. Since then she had been blind. Her parents died in the same accident, and she was brought up in an orphanage. Lisa was now seventeen.

Lisa was very smart, and she did very well in school. She was always at the top of the class and was well respected by her classmates. But she was a quiet person, and didn't talk much with her

Chapter 1
Lisa's Mission

classmates.

Lisa had a secret she had kept for many years. Since the accident, she had been able to hear the voices of the dead sometimes. At first, Lisa got very scared, but over time she had learned to ignore them. She strongly hoped to hear her parents' voices, but she hadn't been able to communicate with her parents.

Lisa loved her parents very much. She was their only daughter, and they also loved Lisa. Just before

---

WORD LIST

- the dead　熟 死者たち
- at first　熟 最初は
- scared　形 怯えた
- over time　熟 時間と共に
- ignore　動 無視する
- communicate with ～　熟 ～と連絡を取り合う

she died, her mother said to Lisa from the hospital bed next to hers, "You're very special. Don't forget your mission." Lisa still didn't understand what her mother had meant then.

One night, when Lisa was lying on her bed, she heard a woman's voice. "Only you can help me. You are my only hope." Lisa ignored the voice as always, but the voice got louder and louder. She repeated the same words: "Only you can help me. You are my only hope."

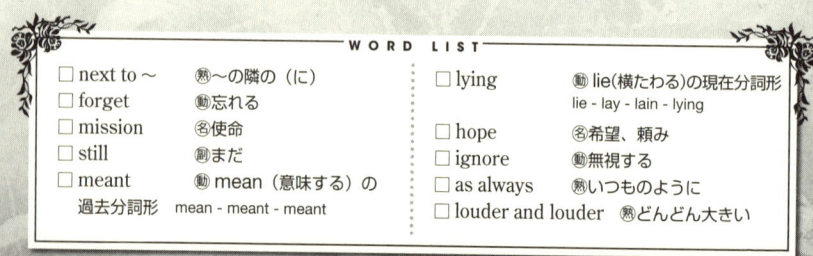

Chapter 1
Lisa's Mission

She couldn't go to sleep, so she finally decided to ask her to stop. "Please don't talk to me anymore. I can't do anything for you. I'm just a normal person. Please ask somebody else. I can't go to sleep."

But the voice didn't stop, and got even louder. It was the first time any voice had repeated itself this many times. Lisa gave up and said, "OK. What do you want? Make it quick. I'm sleepy."

"Thank you..... so much. My name is..... Kay. I lived here until ten years ago, when I was hit by

---

WORD LIST

- decide to V 熟 Vすることを決定する
- anymore 副もはや、これ以上
- else 副その他に
- give up 熟諦める
- be hit by lightning 熟雷に打たれる

lightning and died," the voice said. "I can't leave this world because I have something to tell Sister Mary."

Lisa got curious, and started listening. The voice continued, "Sister Mary was like my mother. She was very good to me, but I was a bad girl, and I was always playing tricks on her. The day before I died, I hid her necklace. When she couldn't find the necklace, she was very upset and searched everywhere. Later I learned it was a present from her dead mother."

WORD LIST

- curious 形物を知りたがる、好奇心の強い
- continue 動続ける
- like ~ 前~のような
- play tricks on ~ 熟~にいたずらをする
- hid 動hide（隠す）の過去形
  hide - hid - hidden
- upset 形混乱した
- search 動捜す
- everywhere 副いたるところで

"The next day after school, I was going to apologize and tell her where I had hidden the necklace, but then that terrible thunderstorm came. When I was running home in the rain, I was hit by lightning. I want you to tell her the place I hid the necklace, please."

Lisa felt very sorry for Kay, and decided to help her. Kay told her that the necklace was in an unused fireplace in the basement, and Lisa promised to tell Sister Mary about it the next morning. "Thank you

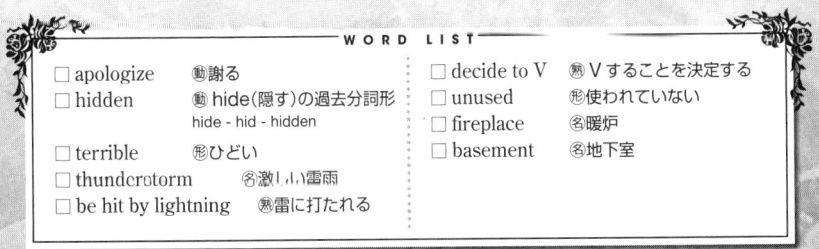

― WORD LIST ―

☐ apologize	動謝る
☐ hidden	動 hide(隠す)の過去分詞形 hide - hid - hidden
☐ terrible	形ひどい
☐ thunderstorm	名激しい雷雨
☐ be hit by lightning	熟雷に打たれる
☐ decide to V	熟 V することを決定する
☐ unused	形使われていない
☐ fireplace	名暖炉
☐ basement	名地下室

very much. Now I can leave this world," Kay said, and she was gone.

The next morning, Lisa went to Sister Mary and told her the story, and Sister Mary found her necklace in the fireplace. She looked Lisa in the eye. Her eyes were filled with tears.

"Now, Lisa, you know what you should do. You are very special. You have a mission."

To be continued

WORD LIST
- fireplace　名暖炉
- filled with ~　熟～でいっぱいで
- tear　名涙
- mission　名使命
- continue　動続ける

LISA
the Teenage Channeler

Chapter 2
Mother's Last message

Mother's Last message

Lisa's mother, Sara, and Sister Mary were born in the same year in the same neighborhood. They were best friends. Sara also had the ability to hear the dead. She kept it a secret, but when she was seventeen, she told Mary about her ability.

"Thank you for sharing your secret with me. I have always thought you are a special person. What are you going to do with your ability?"

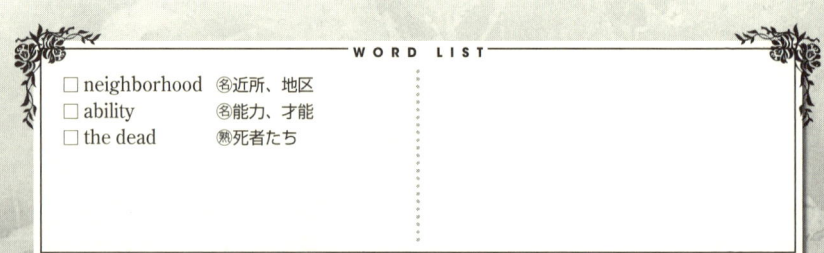

WORD LIST

- neighborhood 名近所、地区
- ability 名能力、才能
- the dead 熟死者たち

Chapter 2
Mother's Last message

Sara didn't know how to answer. She had always ignored the voices because she didn't want to have anything to do with them.

"There must be a reason God gave you the ability. I think you should help those dead people who can't help themselves. Those people might not be able to leave this world because they still have something left to do here. You have to help them," Mary insisted.

From that day, Sara helped dead people leave this world. She helped hundreds of people. She delivered

---

WORD LIST

- ignore 動無視する
- not ..... have anything to do with 〜 熟〜とは一切関わりがない
- still 副まだ
- insist 動主張する、言い張る
- hundreds of 〜 熟何百もの〜
- deliver 動配達する、届ける

LISA
Mother's Last message

messages to their family members and friends. She felt very happy to be able to help them, and it became her mission in life.

She got married to Dan, Lisa's father, but she kept her ability a secret from him. They had a beautiful daughter, and they named her Lisa. When Sara held her daughter in her arms, she knew somehow she would have the same ability as hers. She was going to tell Lisa about her ability and her mission when she was old enough.

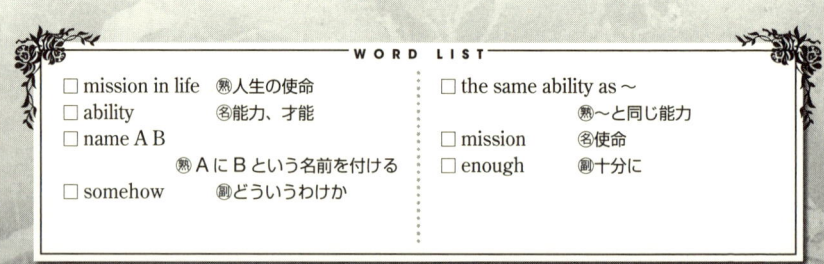

Chapter 2
Mother's Last message

One day Sara began to hear a very strange and scary voice. "Stop what you are doing, or I will kill you." It was a man's voice, and repeated itself almost every night for weeks. Sara was terrified by the voice, and was very tired because she couldn't get enough sleep.

One morning, she was driving with Lisa and Dan in the car. When she came to a curve, she suddenly felt dizzy and passed out. The car went through a fence and rolled over. An ambulance arrived and

---

WORD LIST

☐ scary	形恐ろしい	☐ feel dizzy	熟めまいがする feel - felt - felt
☐ almost	副ほとんど		
☐ terrified	形怯えた	☐ pass out	熟意識を失う
☐ get enough sleep	熟ぐっすり眠る	☐ roll over	熟転がる
☐ curve	名カーブ	☐ ambulance	名救急車
☐ suddenly	副突然		

LISA
Mother's Last message

they were taken to a hospital. Dan died immediately. Sara and Lisa were seriously injured. The next morning Lisa was a little better, but Sara was worse.

The doctor said to her, "I'm very sorry, but you're not going to live long. Do you want to see your daughter one last time?" She said yes, and the nurses pushed her bed next to Lisa's. Then she delivered her own message to Lisa just before she passed away.

"You are very special. You have a mission." She couldn't say any more. She had stopped breathing.

To be continued

WORD LIST

- die immediately　熟即死する
- be seriously injured　熟重傷を負う
- next to ~　熟~の隣の（に）
- deliver　動配達する、届ける
- pass away　熟亡くなる
- mission　名使命
- any more　熟もはや、これ以上
- breathe　動呼吸する
- continue　動続ける

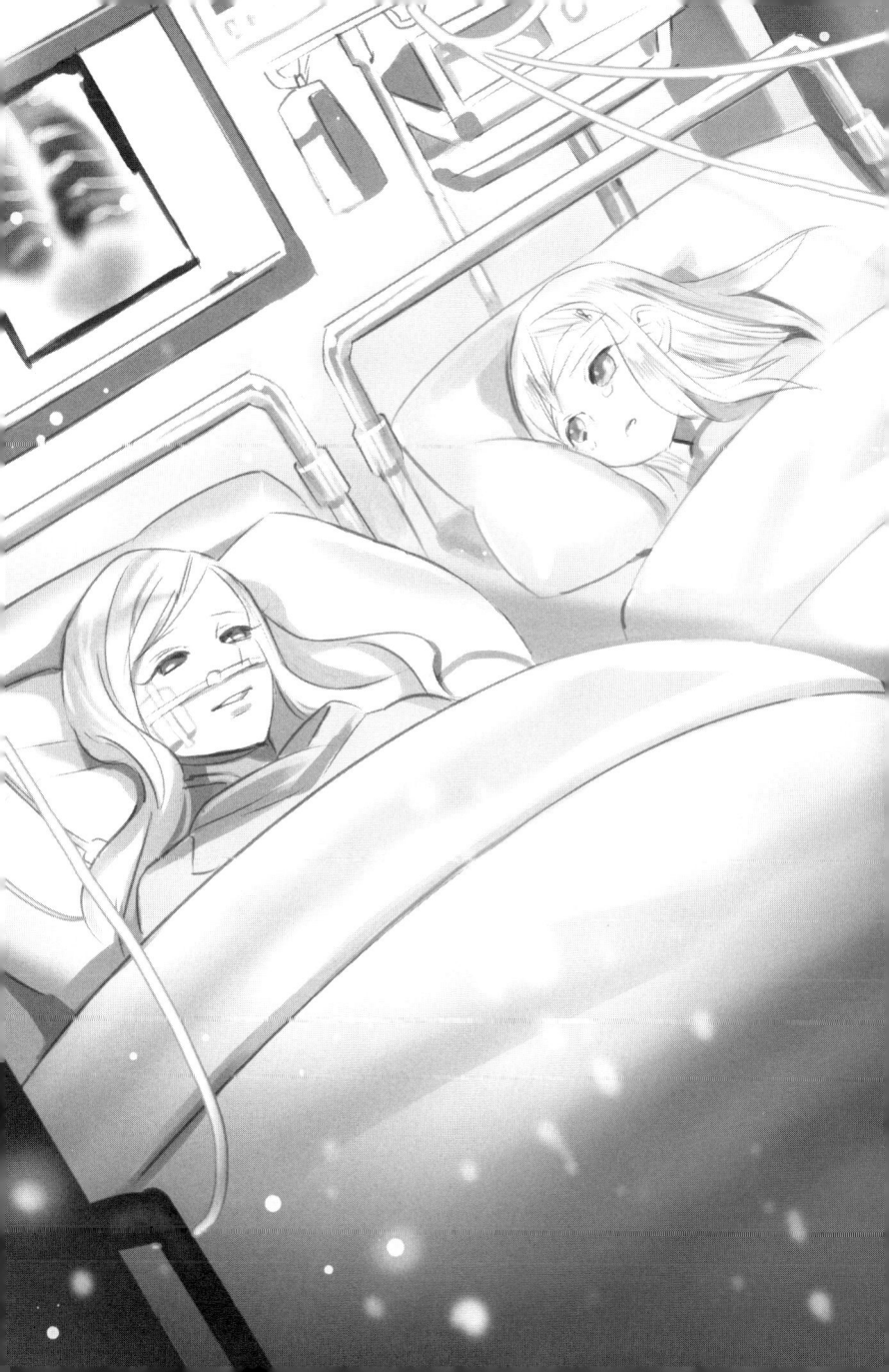

LISA
the Teenage Channeler

Chapter
3
The Voice from the Well

The Voice from the Well

Although Lisa was blind, she had very beautiful eyes. Boys often asked her out on dates, but she always said no. She usually went straight back to the orphanage, and talked with Sister Mary over a cup of tea.

After she told Sister Mary about her ability, they often talked about Lisa's mother, Sara. They talked about what she did to help the dead, and about how

---

WORD LIST

- well　名井戸
- blind　形盲目の
- ask ~ out on a date　熟〜をデートに誘う
- go back to ~　熟〜に帰る
- orphanage　名児童養護施設
- ability　名能力、才能
- talk about ~　熟〜について話す
- the dead　熟死者たち

Chapter 3
The Voice from the Well

Lisa could help dead people.

One night, Lisa heard a voice saying, "Please help me." It was a little boy and his voice was echoing. Lisa asked the boy,

"What do you want me to do? Where are you?"

"My name is David. I'm in the well in the forest. I came here alone. I found this well and fell in. Nobody found me, so I'm still here. It's dark and cold here. Please let my mother know I'm here. I want my mommy." He began to cry.

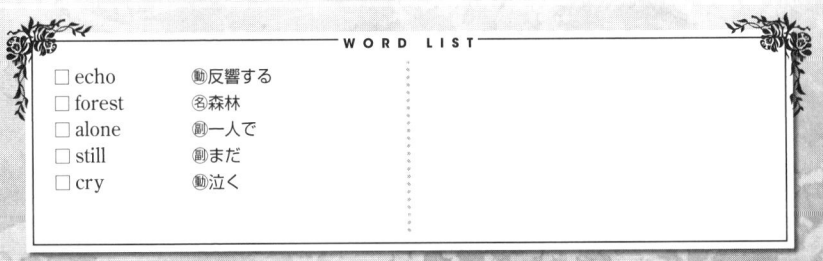

WORD LIST
- echo 動反響する
- forest 名森林
- alone 副一人で
- still 副まだ
- cry 動泣く

LISA
The Voice from the Well

Lisa knew he didn't realize he was dead. "OK, just wait for a little bit. I'll tell your mother where you are tomorrow morning. Where is the well, and what is the name of your mother?"

The following morning, she asked Sister Mary to search on the Internet for a missing boy. She found that a boy named David had been missing for about a year. His mother, Caroline, lived on the other side of the town. Sister Mary drove Lisa to her house.

When Caroline saw Lisa, she didn't know why a

WORD LIST

- realize 動理解する
- wait for ～ 熟～を待つ
- a little bit 熟少し
- well 名井戸
- search 動捜す
- on the Internet 熟インターネットで
- missing 形行方不明の

Chapter 3
The Voice from the Well

teenage girl was visiting her, but when she saw Sister Mary, she thought they had come to sell her a Bible. "We are here to talk with you about your son, David." Lisa said, and Caroline let them in and made them tea.

Lisa told her the story about David's voice. Caroline got very upset. She didn't want to believe her son was dead, and got very angry. She asked them to leave. Lisa was very sad. She was only trying to help David's mother, but she got such a cold

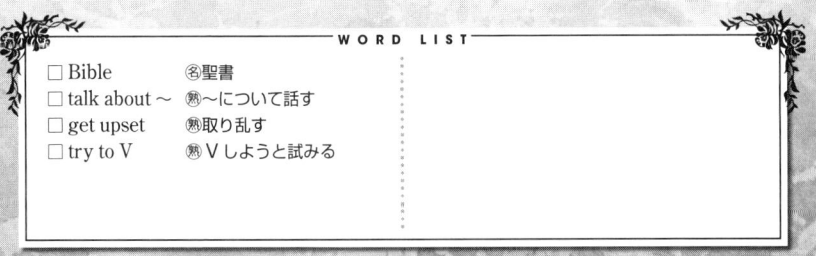

WORD LIST
- Bible ㊂聖書
- talk about ～ ㊃～について話す
- get upset ㊃取り乱す
- try to V ㊃V しようと試みる

reaction. She began to cry.

"Don't be so sad, Lisa. You're doing the right thing. It's the mission God gave you. You have to keep delivering messages. That's a job only you can do. You're very special," said Sister Mary.

Later that afternoon, Caroline was thinking about what Lisa had said. Finally, she decided to call the police and ask them to search the well in the forest. The police found David's body in the well.

That evening, Lisa was lying on her bed, because

Chapter 3
The Voice from the Well

she didn't want to do anything. She was so sad. "Why do I have to do this, Mother? Is this mission to deliver messages so important?" she was saying to herself.

Suddenly she heard Sister Mary calling her from downstairs. She said there was a visitor. It was Caroline. "I'm very sorry I got angry at you this morning. You were right. The police found David's body in the well. I'm very sorry I doubted you," Caroline said, her eyes filled with tears. "Can you still hear David's voice? Is he here?"

WORD LIST

☐ important	形大切な	☐ tear	名涙
☐ say to oneself	熟(心の中で)考える、独り言を言う	☐ still	副まだ
☐ suddenly	副突然		
☐ downstairs	名階下		
☐ doubt	動疑う		
☐ filled with ~	熟~でいっぱいで		

"I'm sure he's here beside you, and he can hear you. You should let him know he is dead. He has to move on," said Lisa.

"David, I want to hold you again, but I can't. Mommy and you are in different worlds now. Someday Mommy will see you in your world. Until then, Mommy has to say goodbye. Say hi to Grandma. Don't forget I will always love you."

Then Lisa heard David's voice saying, "I love you, too, Mommy. Goodbye."

To be continued

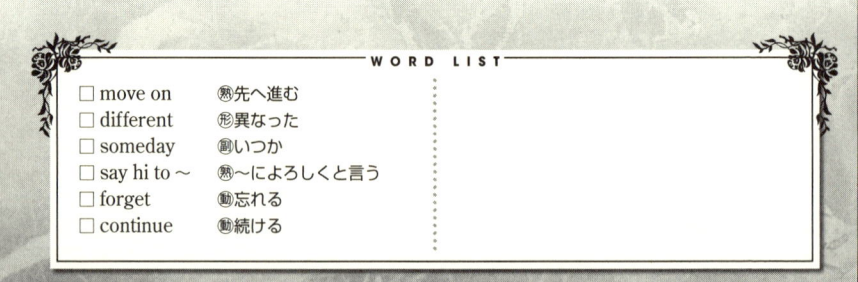

WORD LIST

- move on — 熟 先へ進む
- different — 形 異なった
- someday — 副 いつか
- say hi to ~ — 熟 〜によろしくと言う
- forget — 動 忘れる
- continue — 動 続ける

LISA
the Teenage Channeler

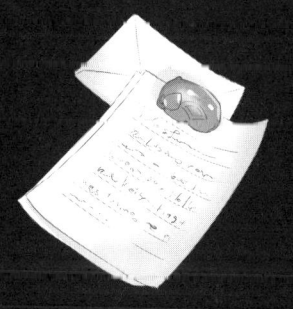

Chapter
4
Time Travel

Time Travel

Winter was very cold that year. It snowed a lot more than usual, and the children in the orphanage were very glad that they could play with snow in the yard.

Lisa was at the kitchen table waiting for Sister Mary to make tea for her. "I got a special Indian herb tea today. It has many herbs that are good for your health. Please try it," said Sister Mary.

WORD LIST

- a lot more than usual (熟)いつもよりずっと多く
- orphanage (名)児童養護施設
- wait for ~ (熟)~を待つ
- herb tea (熟)ハーブティー

Chapter 4
Time Travel

After drinking the tea, Lisa started to feel dizzy, and she fell asleep. She started dreaming. The dream was very real, and in the dream she could see. She was on a beach. In front of her stood her classmate, Emily.

"Hi, Emily, I didn't expect to see you here. How are you?" asked Lisa, but Emily couldn't hear or see her. Lisa was invisible to her. Emily put a piece of paper on the sand and weighed it down with a stone, then she started to walk forward and then into the

---

WORD LIST

- feel dizzy 　(熟)めまいがする
  feel - felt - felt
- fall asleep 　(熟)(ぐっすり)寝入る
  fall - fell - fallen
- in front of ~ 　(熟)~の前で(に)
- invisible 　(形)見えない
- weigh ~ down 　(熟)~を圧する、押し下げる
- forward 　(副)前へ

sea. Finally a wave swallowed her, and Lisa couldn't see her anymore.

Lisa read what was written on the paper. It said, "I didn't steal the money. I hate everyone, and everyone hates me. Nobody believed me. I don't want to live anymore." Lisa walked back to town and learned from a newspaper that she was having a vision of six months into the future.

Lisa didn't understand why Emily had to die, and she couldn't believe that Emily had stolen money.

WORD LIST

- swallow　動飲み込む
- anymore　副もはや、これ以上
- steal　動盗む
  steal - stole - stolen
- vision　名映像

"She couldn't have done it. She is a very nice and honest person," Lisa thought to herself. Then she felt dizzy again, and suddenly she was back at the table with Sister Mary.

Although Lisa felt she had been away for a very long time, Sister Mary said she hadn't noticed Lisa fall asleep. They learned the Indian herb tea had the power to send Lisa into the future. Lisa drank the tea again, but this time she had just a little bit. She felt dizzy again, and when she opened her eyes, it was

---

WORD LIST

☐ think to oneself	熟 心の中で考える	☐ notice	動 気付く
☐ feel dizzy	熟 めまいがする feel - felt - felt	☐ fall asleep	熟 (ぐっすり) 寝入る fall - fell - fallen
☐ suddenly	副 突然	☐ herb tea	熟 ハーブティー
☐ away	副 離れて、不在で	☐ a little bit	熟 少し
☐ for a long time	熟 長い間		

spring.

She was in a classroom in the morning. Some girls were talking. One girl said, "Do you know where the money for the class trip is kept? It's kept in Mrs. Green's office. It's kept in her desk drawer, and her office door and her drawer don't have locks."

Another girl said, "But we might get caught. Mrs. Green will probably suspect us first."

"Then we should make Mrs. Green suspect somebody else, like Emily. Her family is poor, and she doesn't talk much. Nobody will doubt it," another girl said.

During the lunch break, they took the money, and secretly put some small bills and the envelope into Emily's bag.

Mrs. Green was very angry, and asked the class about the money. When nobody answered, she asked everybody to put their bags on their desks. She found the envelope and the bills in Emily's bag. Mrs. Green asked Emily where the rest of the money was,

---

WORD LIST

- doubt 動疑う
- secretly 副秘密に
- bill 名紙幣、請求書
- envelope 名封筒
- rest 名残り

but Emily just cried.

After Lisa came back to the present, she talked with Sister Mary about what she could do. They thought the best thing was to make Mrs. Green install locks on her office door and her desk drawer.

One day, after school, Lisa secretly went into Mrs. Green's office and got some things out of her drawer and put them on the desk. She also moved some pieces of furniture. The next day, in class, Mrs. Green asked the students what they knew about the incident. Lisa raised her hand and said, "I think it might be a thief from outside. I think you should install locks on the office door and the drawer. It's too dangerous without locks."

Mrs. Green was very surprised that the usually quiet girl gave her opinion in front of everybody, but she didn't suspect her, and took her suggestion seriously. She installed locks in her office.

The next time Lisa visited the beach again, after drinking the Indian herb tea, she saw Emily walking

---

WORD LIST

□ incident	⑧事件	□ in front of ~	㊹~の前で（に）
□ raise	⑩上げる	□ suspect	⑩怪しいと思う、容疑をかける
□ thief	⑧泥棒		
□ too ~	⑩あまりにも~	□ suggestion	⑧提案
□ dangerous	㊙危険な	□ seriously	⑩深刻に
□ opinion	⑧意見	□ herb tea	㊹ハーブティー

LISA
Time Travel

with her mother.

They were smiling at each other and looked very happy. They were looking at a beautiful sunset. Lisa stood beside them and watched the sun sink into the horizon.

To be continued

WORD LIST

- each other — 熟 お互い（に）
- sink — 動 沈む
  sink - sank - sunk (sunken)
- the horizon — 熟 地平線
- continue — 動 続ける

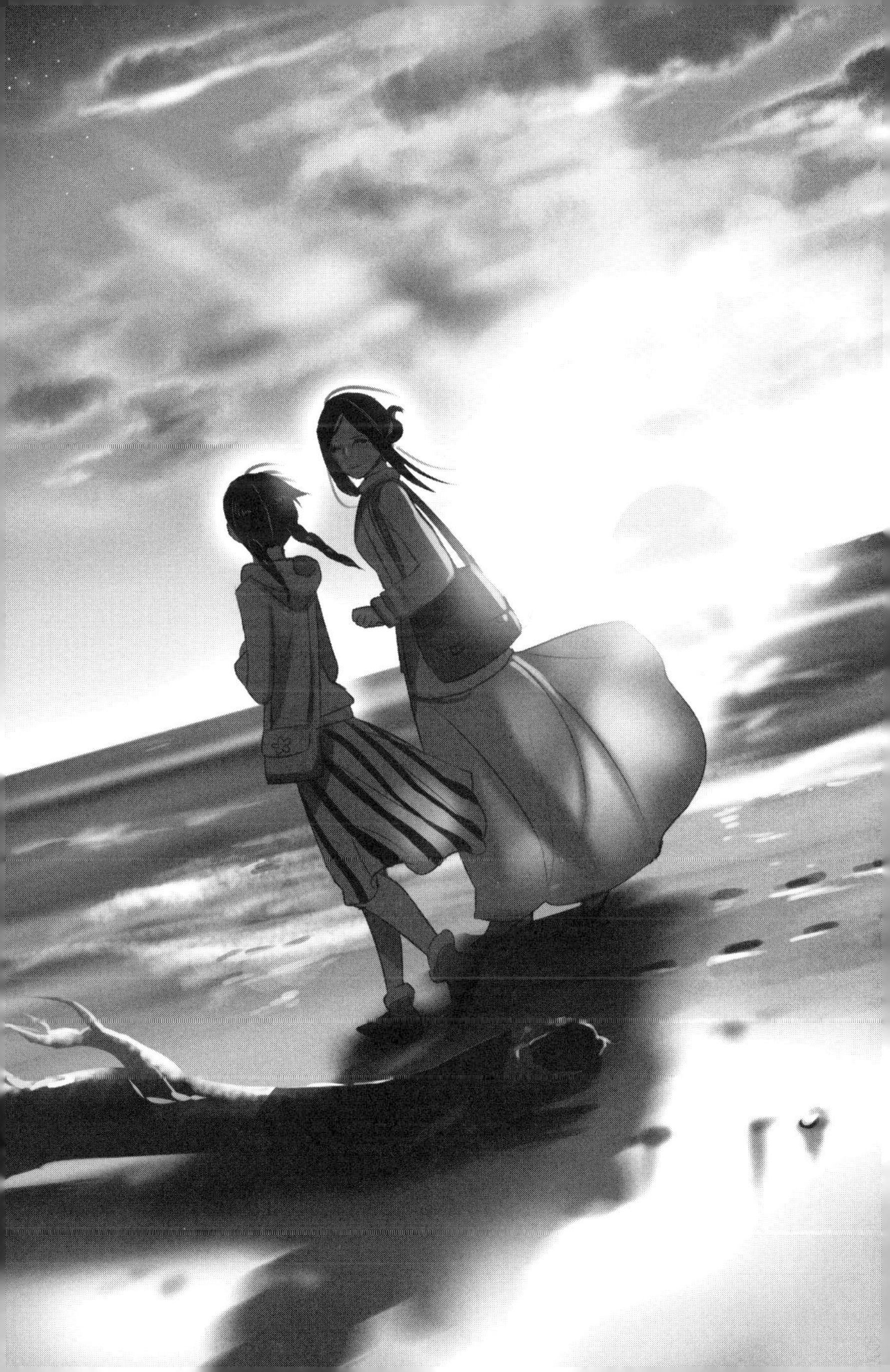

LISA
the Teenage Channeler

Chapter
5
Murderer in Disguise

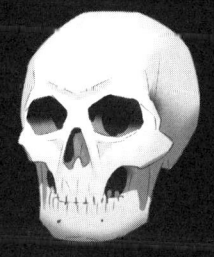

Murderer in Disguise

Ben Garner, the chemistry teacher, was in his forties, but he looked much younger. His class was very interesting and he was very popular with his students. Lisa also liked him, but not because his class was fun, but because his voice sounded like her dead father's.

When he was alive, Lisa's father often told her bedtime stories. Lisa felt like she was listening to her

---

WORD LIST

- murderer 名殺人者
- disguise 名変装
- chemistry 名化学
- in one's forties 熟(年齢が) 40 代で
- sound like ~ 熟〜に思われる
- alive 形生きている
- bedtime story 熟(子どもを寝かし付ける時にする) おとぎ話
- feel like ~ 熟〜のような気がする
  feel - felt - felt

Chapter 5
Murderer in Disguise

father's stories in Ben's class. Lisa always pictured her father's face in the class. It was like her father had come back and was talking to her.

Lisa sometimes visited Ben's office to ask questions, not because she didn't understand his lesson, but because she just wanted to talk with him.

One afternoon, he said to her, "If you're so interested in science, you should try out the professional equipment that I have at home. I'll teach you how to use it. Don't worry. School's over now,

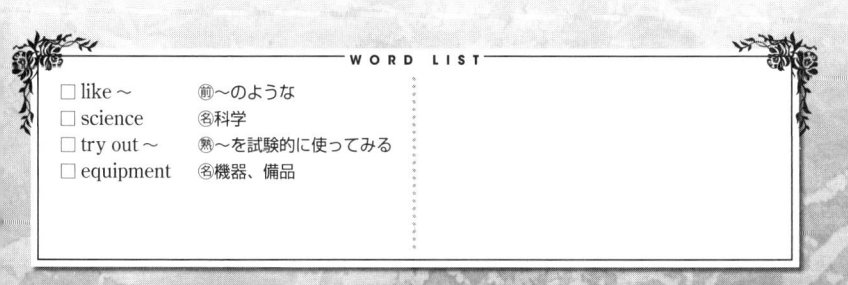

WORD LIST
- like ~　　前 ～のような
- science　　名 科学
- try out ~　　熟 ～を試験的に使ってみる
- equipment　　名 機器、備品

and I have nothing to do this afternoon, so why don't you come to my house?"

"I should call Sister Mary and ask for her permission," Lisa said.

"Don't worry. I'll drive you home by five. You don't need to bother her," Ben said.

Lisa nodded, and they got in Ben's old car, and headed for Ben's home.

Lisa felt like she was riding in a car with her father, and she and Ben had a lot of interesting things to talk

Chapter 5
Murderer in Disguise

about. When the conversation stopped, Lisa heard the voice of a girl.

"Run! Run for your life! Run! Run for your life! This man is dangerous!"

Lisa didn't know what to do. She was trapped in the car with Ben. She couldn't ask the girl anything because Ben was next to her. The voice didn't stop, and kept repeating the same words. Lisa started to get scared.

They arrived at Ben's house, and Ben seated Lisa

WORD LIST

- conversation 名会話
- for one's life 熟必死で
- dangerous 形危険な
- be trapped in ~ 熟~に閉じ込められる
- next to ~ 熟~の隣の（に）
- scared 形怯えた

LISA
Murderer in Disguise

at the living room table.

"I'll make you some tea," he said, and went to the kitchen.

The voice was still there, so Lisa asked her in a low voice,

"What do you mean? Who is he?"

"Thank God! You can hear me. Run. He's a murderer." the voice said.

"Murderer? Who do you mean?" asked Lisa.

"That guy. Ben Garner. He killed me. He put

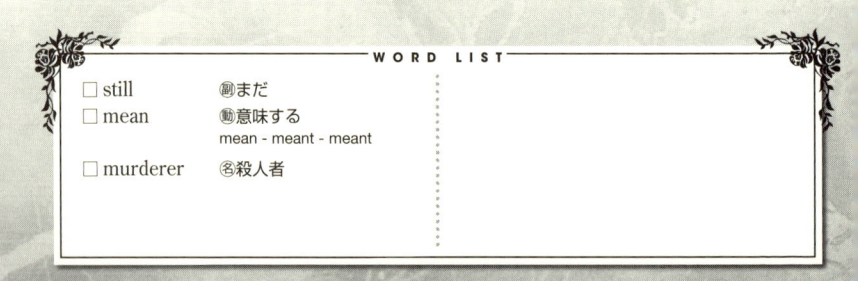

Chapter 5
Murderer in Disguise

something in my tea and I fell asleep, and then he..." she was crying. "After he killed me, he dissolved my body in some chemical, and buried my bones in the backyard. Run now. Run for your life. Don't drink the tea," the voice warned.

Lisa couldn't believe what she was hearing, but she thought she should ask somebody for help anyway.

Ben came back to the room with the tea and sat at the table. Lisa said she wanted to use the bathroom,

---

WORD LIST

- fall asleep 熟(ぐっすり)寝入る
  fall - fell - fallen
- cry 動泣く
- dissolve 動溶かす
- body 名体、遺体
- chemical 名化学薬品
- bury 動埋める、葬る
- for one's life 熟必死で
- warn 動警告する
- anyway 副ともかく

and she went, her cell phone in her pocket. She tried to act as normal as possible.

In the bathroom, she sent a voicemail to Sister Mary, saying that she wanted her to call the police and ask them to send officers to Ben's house.

She went back to the table, and talked as long as possible without drinking the tea.

"Why don't you drink some tea? It's good," Ben said. She had no choice. She drank just a little bit, and said, "Um……. I'm sorry, Mr. Garner, but this tea

Chapter 5
Murderer in Disguise

is a little too strong for me. Could you make this a little weaker?" This was her way of buying time, but she began to get drowsy because of the tea she had already drunk, and finally fell asleep.

Ben came back with a pair of scissors, and he cut a lock of Lisa's hair, which he put in a bottle. Then he tied her to the chair with a rope.

When Lisa woke up, she could hear Ben breathing just beside her; he was holding a knife.

The girl's voice was saying, "Wake up! Wake up!"

WORD LIST

☐ too strong for me	熟 私には濃過ぎる	☐ a lock of hair	熟 ひとふさの髪
☐ buy time	熟 時間を稼ぐ	☐ tie	動 結ぶ、しばる
☐ drowsy	形 眠い	☐ breathe	動 呼吸する
☐ fall asleep	熟 (ぐっすり)寝入る fall - fell - fallen		
☐ a pair of scissors	熟 ハサミ一丁		

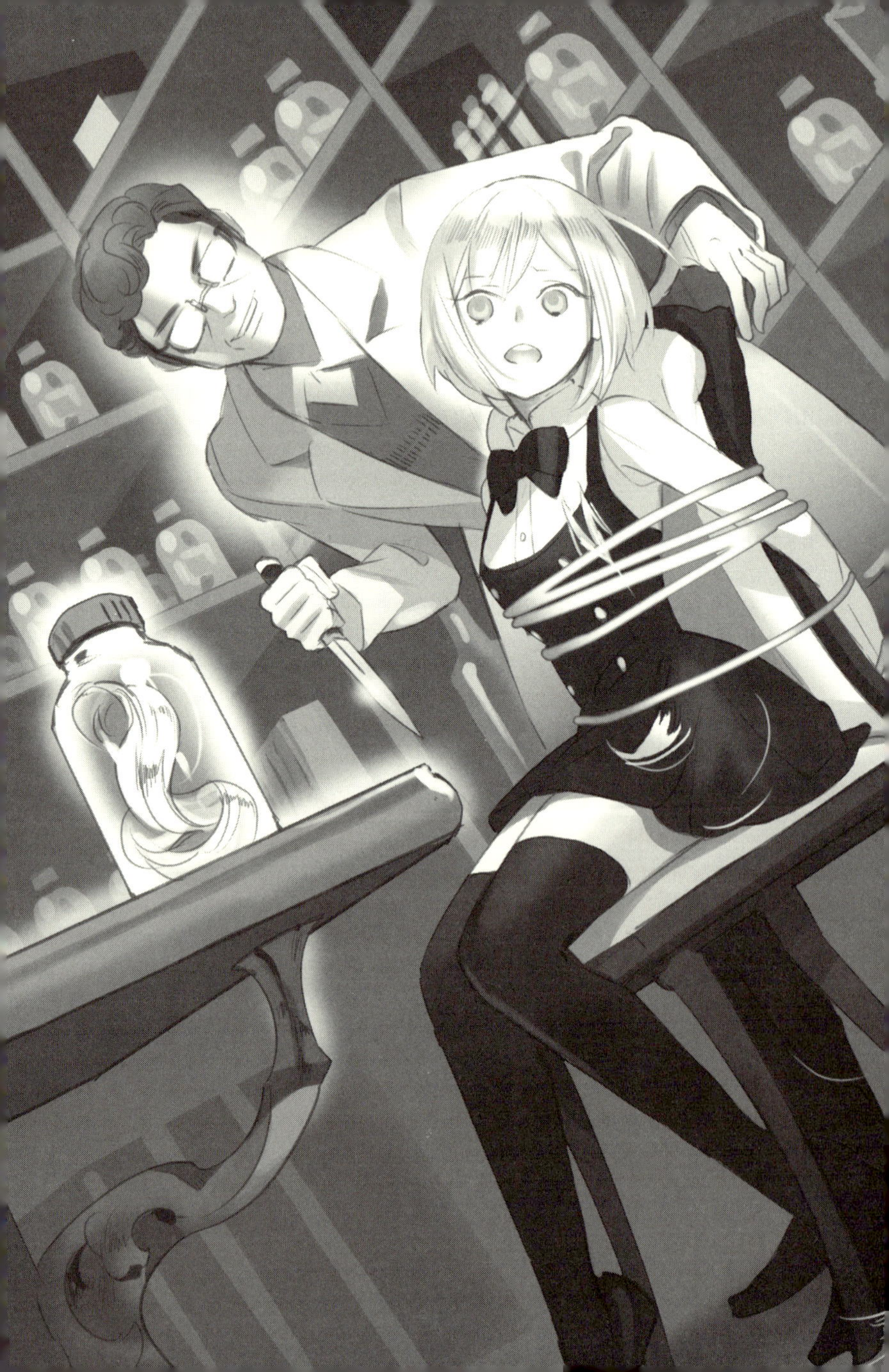

Chapter 5
Murderer in Disguise

"Mother, help me. I don't want to die yet," Lisa said to herself.

Just when Ben held the knife up, Lisa heard a gun shot and Ben cry out. The bullet came through the window and hit Ben's shoulder, and he fell to the floor. Several officers broke into the house through the door, and rushed toward Lisa and untied her. They arrested Ben.

"He might have killed another girl," Lisa told the officers. They searched the house and found another

---

WORD LIST

- say to oneself 熟（心の中で）考える、独り言を言う
- cry out 熟叫ぶ
- bullet 名弾丸
- come through ~ 熟~を通り抜ける
- officer 名警官、役人
- break into ~ 熟~に押し入る break - broke - broken
- rush 動急いで行く
- arrest 動逮捕する
- search 動捜す

LISA
Murderer in Disguise

bottle with somebody's hair in it, and later they found the bones of a girl buried in the backyard.

After a DNA test, it turned out that the girl's name was Adeline Brown, and she had been missing for a year. She was seventeen when she disappeared.

Lisa went to put flowers on Adeline's grave. She wanted to thank her, but she couldn't hear her voice anymore. Lisa hoped Adeline had finally found peace and had gone to the other world.

To be continued

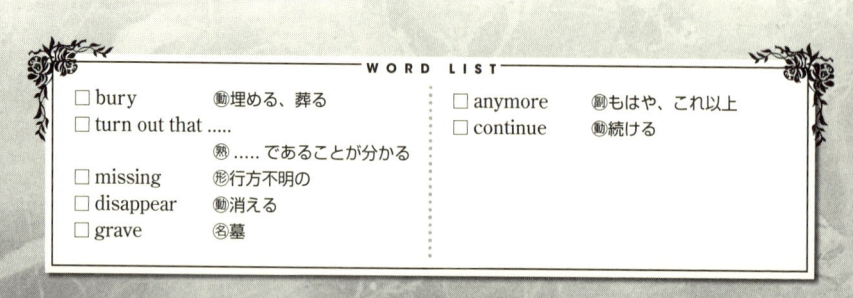

WORD LIST

- bury 動埋める、葬る
- turn out that ..... 熟 ..... であることが分かる
- missing 形行方不明の
- disappear 動消える
- grave 名墓
- anymore 副もはや、これ以上
- continue 動続ける

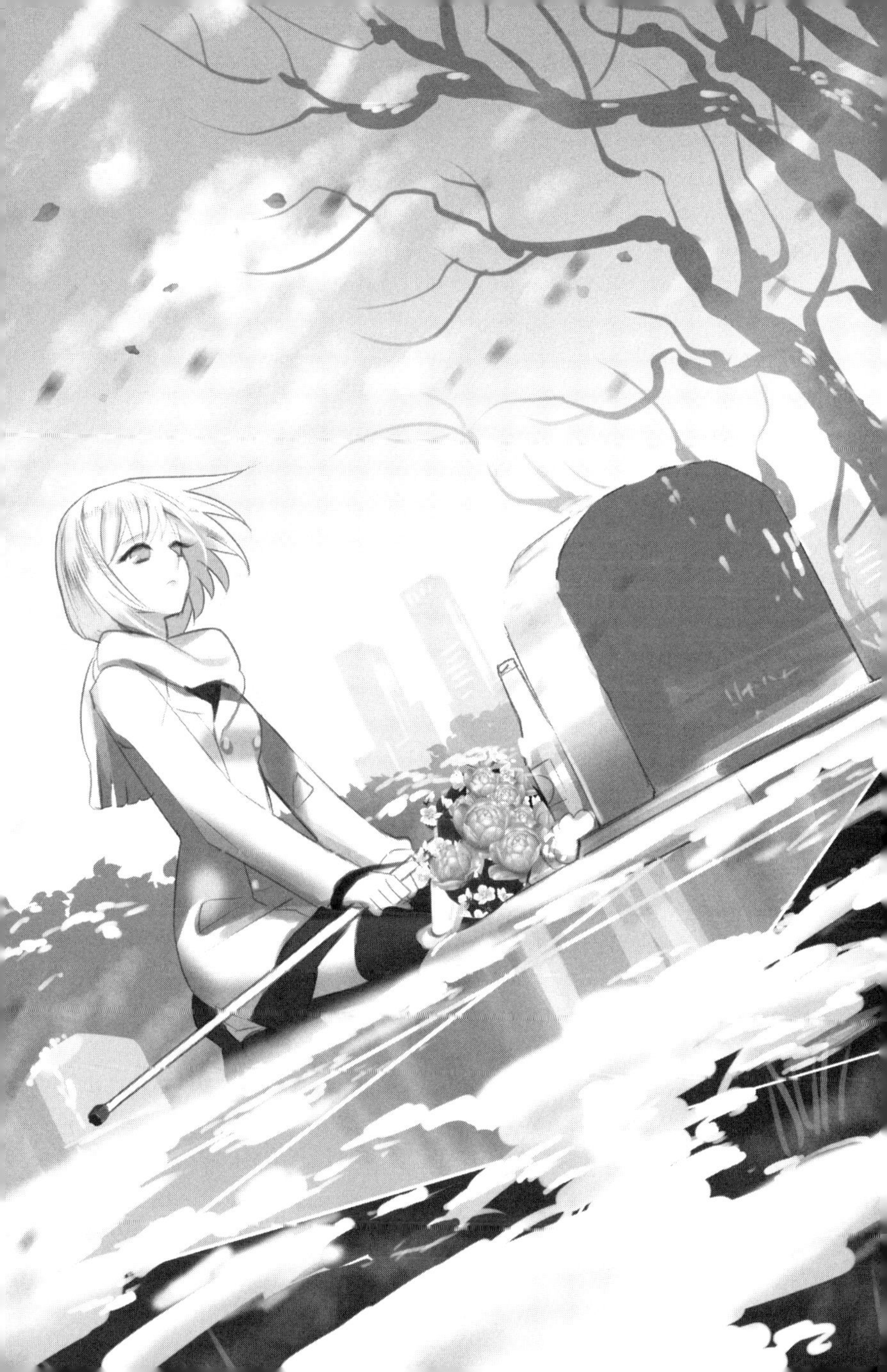

LISA
the Teenage Channeler

Chapter 6
Ken's Secret

Ken's Secret

Ken Black was eighteen years old. He was very handsome and did very well in school. Many girls wanted to talk with him, but he didn't seem very interested in girls.

Ken had a shameful secret. When he was ten years old, for no particular reason he wanted to see a dead body. He secretly went to a graveyard, found a new grave and dug until he found a coffin. He broke

Chapter 6
Ken's Secret

open the lid, and saw the face of a girl of his age. Then he got scared and ran away.

After that, he began to see the ghost of the girl everywhere. He felt very guilty and even tried to commit suicide several times. He couldn't tell his secret to anybody because he didn't want anybody to know he had done such a bad thing. The girl's ghost seemed to be talking to him, but he couldn't hear her. He thought she was angry, so he ignored her.

One day when Lisa was sitting on a bench in the

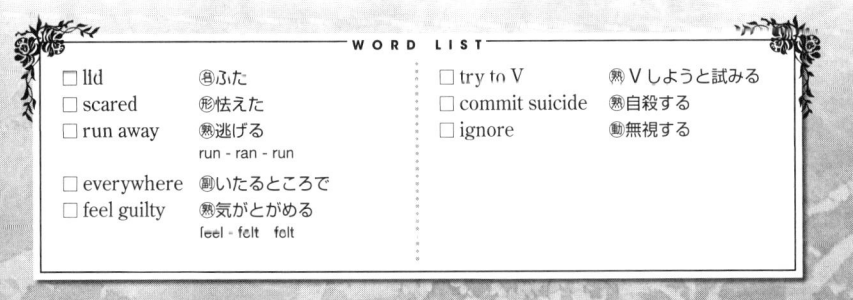

WORD LIST

- lld — 名ふた
- scared — 形怯えた
- run away — 熟逃げる run - ran - run
- everywhere — 副いたるところで
- feel guilty — 熟気がとがめる feel - felt felt
- try to V — 熟 V しようと試みる
- commit suicide — 熟自殺する
- ignore — 動無視する

LISA
Ken's Secret

school yard, she heard a girl's voice. She was talking to somebody else. "Please help my father. After I died, he started drinking a lot. He lost his job and his home, and now he is living on the street." She was clearly not talking to Lisa, but instead, talking to Ken, who was sitting beside Lisa.

"He thinks it was his fault that I died. I asked him to go and buy me an ice cream, and he left me at home alone. That was when that terrible man came and killed me. It was not my father's fault. A man

---

WORD LIST

- else 副その他に
- a lot 熟よく、とても
- clearly 副明らかに
- instead 副その代わりに
- fault 名責任、罪
- alone 副一人で
- terrible 形ひどい

Chapter 6
Ken's Secret

named Mark killed me. It wasn't a burglar. He was my mother's lover. It was Mark who killed me," the girl continued.

Lisa thought she had to do something about this, and decided to talk to the person sitting next to her, Ken.

"Excuse me. Can you hear what she's saying?" Lisa asked Ken, and he was very surprised.

"You see her too?" Ken said.

"No, I'm blind, but I can hear her. My name is Lisa

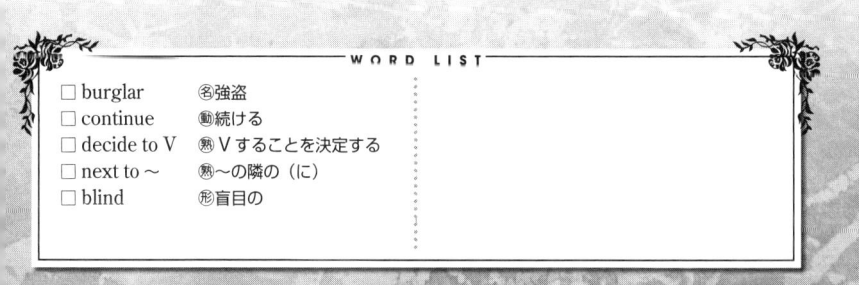

WORD LIST

- □ burglar ㊔強盗
- □ continue ㊔続ける
- □ decide to V ㊔Vすることを決定する
- □ next to ～ ㊔～の隣の（に）
- □ blind ㊔盲目の

LISA
Ken's Secret

White. It might be hard to believe, but I can hear the dead, and I help them find peace. The ghost you see, she's giving you a very important message."

"She's not angry with me? I can't hear anything. I only see her. She's been haunting me for a long time. Maybe that's my fault."

"Well, anyway, I think we should help her. If you can't hear her, I can help you. She doesn't seem angry with you. What did you do to her?"

"I did a bad thing when I was a kid. Anyway, if I

WORD LIST

- the dead　熟 死者たち
- important　形 大切な
- haunt　動 つきまとう
- for a long time　熟 長い間
- maybe　副 たぶん
- fault　名 責任、罪
- anyway　副 ともかく

Chapter 6
Ken's Secret

can help her, I want to. Could you please help me?"

Lisa told the ghost that Ken couldn't hear her and that Lisa was going to tell Ken her message, and so the ghost told Lisa the story.

"My mother was having an affair. I was never very close to my mother, and she hated me. Her lover, Mark, also hated me and my father. He wanted to kill us in order to keep my mother to himself. But, because my father went out, only I was killed that day. The police couldn't find any clues. They thought

---
WORD LIST

- and so 熟 それゆえ、それで
- have an affair 熟 浮気をする
- very 副〈否定文で〉あまり
- close to ~ 熟 ~と親しい仲で
- keep ~ to oneself 熟 ~を独占する、秘密にする
- the police 熟 警察
- clue 名 手がかり

LISA
Ken's Secret

it was a burglar..." the girl started to cry.

Ken and Lisa went to the library, and Ken searched on the Internet. He found out that the girl who had been killed eight years ago was Erica Telford. She was ten years old when she was killed.

They went downtown to look for her father, and found him, Frank Telford, now living on the streets. He had a long dirty beard and was holding a whiskey bottle in one hand. He looked very unhealthy.

When they were about to talk to him, he suddenly

WORD LIST

- burglar 名強盗
- cry 動泣く
- search 動捜す
- on the Internet 熟インターネットで
- find out that ..... 熟 ..... を見つけ出す
- look for 〜 熟〜を捜す
- beard 名あごひげ
- be about to V 熟まさに V しようとしている
- suddenly 副突然

Chapter 6
Ken's Secret

began to groan. His hand on his chest, he fell down. They called an ambulance, but it was too late. His heart had stopped.

Ken could see his soul was leaving his body. The ghost looked around, not knowing what had happened to him. Then he saw Erica running toward him. She jumped into his arms and embraced him. They smiled at each other, and then disappeared.

Later that day, Lisa and Ken talked about what they should do about the murderer, Mark. They tried

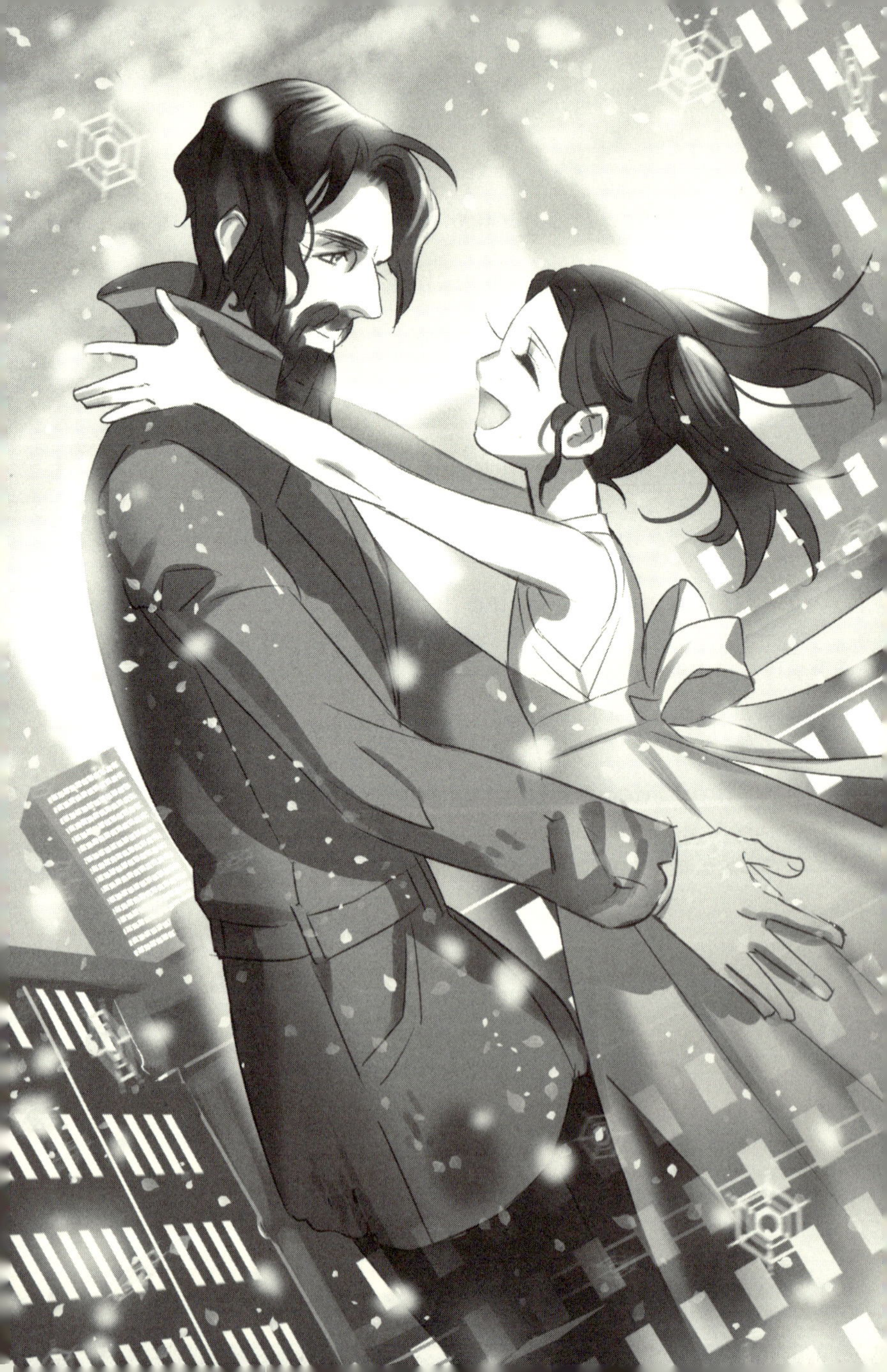

Chapter 6
Ken's Secret

their best to track him down. They continued to do so for several days, and finally found a person named Mark Baldwin, who was a local used-car salesman.

The more time she spent with Ken, the more Lisa began to like him. He was gentle and always considerate of her feelings. It was the first time that Lisa had had feelings for a man. Ken felt the same about Lisa. He liked leading her by the hand, and wished he could keep helping her like that.

Lisa and Ken decided to visit the used-car lot, and

WORD LIST

- track ~ down　熟〜を追いつめる、やっと見つけ出す
- continue　動続ける
- local　形地元の
- gentle　形優しい
- considerate　形思いやりがある
- lead ・ by the hand　熟〜の手を引いてあげる
- like ~　前〜のように
- decide to V　熟Vすることを決定する
- lot　名地所

LISA
Ken's Secret

see what kind of person Mark was. When they arrived there in Ken's car, several police cars were parked in front of the store. They asked an officer what had happened, and learned a woman had been killed there.

It turned out later that the dead woman was Erica's mother. The police suspected her lover, Mark, and arrested him. He confessed to several murders, including Erica's.

"Why do they hate and kill each other like this?

WORD LIST

- park 動駐車させる
- in front of ~ 熟〜の前で（に）
- officer 名警官、役人
- turn out that ..... 熟.....であることが分かる
- the dead 熟死者たち
- the police 熟警察
- suspect 動怪しいと思う、容疑をかける
- arrest 動逮捕する
- confess to ~ 熟〜を白状する
- murder 名殺人
- including ~ 前〜を含めて
- each other 熟お互い（に）

Why can't people be kind? Why did God create a world like this? What am I doing this for?" Lisa cried.

Ken put his arms around her and said, "It's all right, Lisa. You are doing the right thing. All the people you helped left this world, filled with love. You don't have to do this alone anymore. I'll always be with you."

He continued to hold her in his arms as he said this.

To be continued

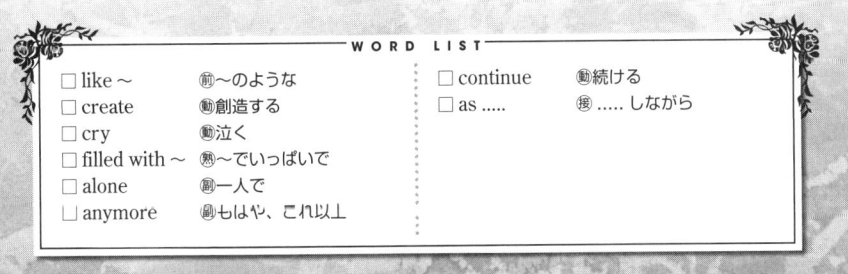

WORD LIST

- like ~ 前 ~のような
- create 動 創造する
- cry 動 泣く
- filled with ~ 熟 ~でいっぱいで
- alone 副 一人で
- anymore 副 もはや、これ以上
- continue 動 続ける
- as ..... 接 ..... しながら

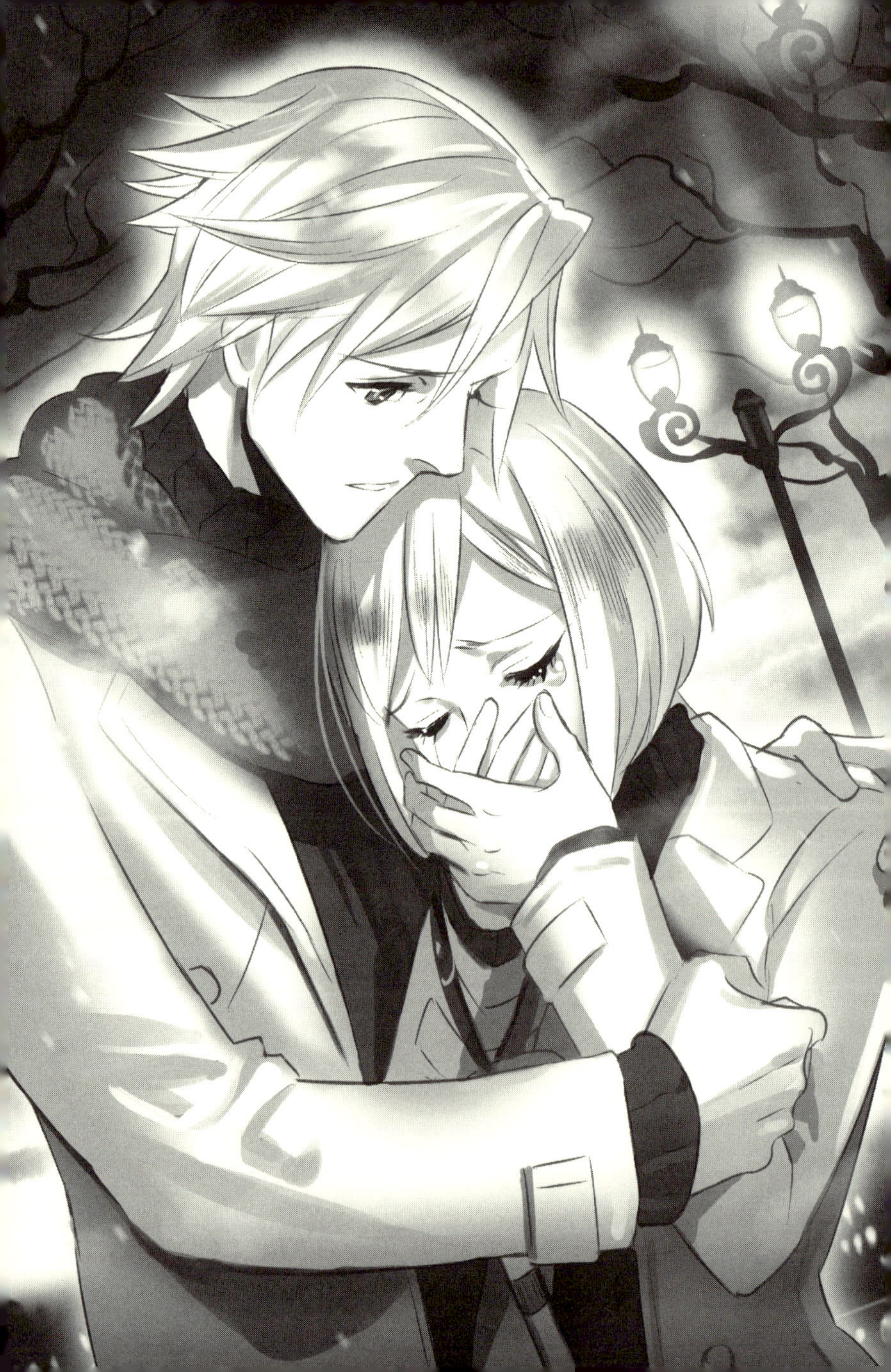

LISA
the Teenage Channeler

Chapter
7
Pine Pond

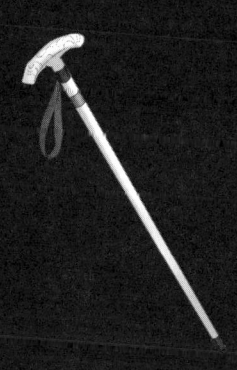

Pine Pond

Lisa and Ken began to help each other out. Ken could see the ghosts, and Lisa could hear them. Lisa and Ken began to fall in love with each other. They were a perfect team.

Together they helped a lot of spirits find peace and leave this world. At first Ken started doing this because he just wanted to help Lisa, but after some time he began to feel he was doing a very important

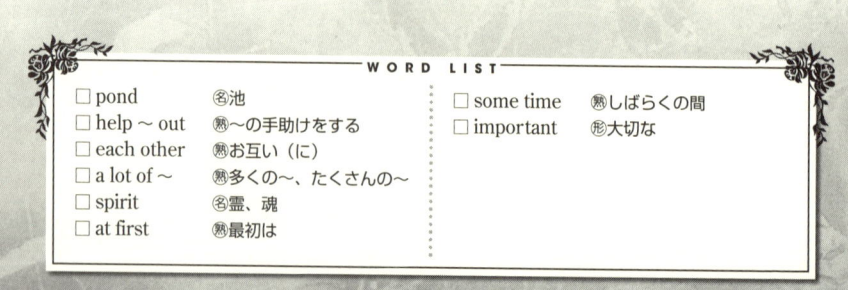

WORD LIST

- pond ㊟池
- help ~ out ㊟~の手助けをする
- each other ㊟お互い（に）
- a lot of ~ ㊟多くの~、たくさんの~
- spirit ㊟霊、魂
- at first ㊟最初は
- some time ㊟しばらくの間
- important ㊟大切な

Chapter 7
Pine Pond

thing to make the world a better place.

One afternoon, when Lisa was walking with Ken, she heard the voice of a child. "Please help me. I'm underwater. I fell from a boat and drowned. Nobody found me. Please come find me at Pine Pond."

Lisa asked his name, and he said his name was Thomas. Lisa and Ken searched the web for the boy, but they couldn't find any information about him.

Pine Pond was just outside the town. People enjoyed boating and fishing there on weekends.

WORD LIST

- make ~ a better place　熟 ～をより良い場所にする
- drown　動 おぼれ死ぬ
- search　動 捜す
- enjoy boating and fishing　熟 船遊びや魚釣りを楽しむ

LISA
Pine Pond

The next afternoon, they went to the pond in Ken's car. Because it was a Wednesday, not many people were there. They parked their car in front of the boat house, and walked to the pier.

Standing on the pier, Lisa called to Thomas. She only heard him say, "Come help me. Come help me." He sounded very weak.

"Can you see anything on the lake?" Lisa asked Ken, but he said he couldn't see anything there.

They decided to rent a boat and go around the

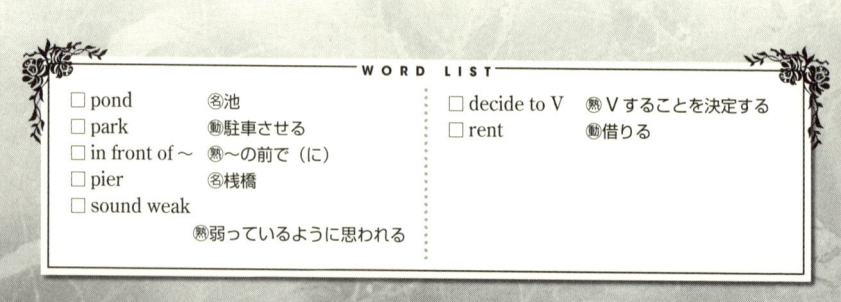

WORD LIST

- pond　名池
- park　動駐車させる
- in front of ～　熟～の前で（に）
- pier　名桟橋
- sound weak　熟弱っているように思われる
- decide to V　熟Vすることを決定する
- rent　動借りる

Chapter 7
Pine Pond

pond to see if they could find where he was.

"You don't have to come. It might be dangerous. If anything happens, I can swim back to the shore, but you..." Ken said.

"I'll go with you. You can't hear his voice, so you need me. I think I'll be safe because I'll be with you, right, tough guy? Please let me go with you," She insisted.

They got into the boat and rowed to the center of the pond. Lisa called to the boy again, but this time

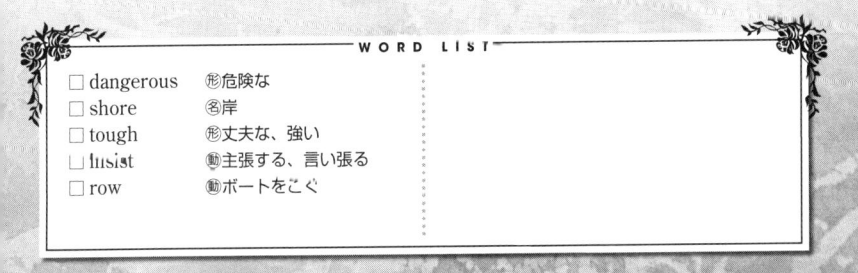

WORD LIST

- dangerous　形危険な
- shore　名岸
- tough　形丈夫な、強い
- insist　動主張する、言い張る
- row　動ボートをこぐ

LISA
Pine Pond

she heard a different voice.

It was a man's voice, and it said, "Stop what you are doing, or I will kill you." The boat suddenly started rocking. Lisa and Ken held on to the rim of the boat. One oar fell off the boat and sank underwater. Water started coming into the boat.

Ken saw their boat was surrounded by black shapes, which looked like small animals. There were hundreds of them.

Ken tried to cling on to Lisa's hand. She felt the

WORD LIST

- different 形異なった
- suddenly 副突然
- rock 動揺れ動く
- rim 名へり、縁
- oar 名オール
- fall off ~ 熟~から離れ落ちる
  fall - fell - fallen
- be surrounded by ~ 熟~に囲まれる
- look like ~ 熟~のように見える
- hundreds of ~ 熟何百もの~
- try to cling on to ~ 熟~にしがみつこうと試みる

Chapter 7
Pine Pond

remaining oar slipping. As she tried to hold onto the oar, she lost her balance and fell into the pond.

Ken saw the black things surround her. He jumped into the water to save her. He was also surrounded by the dark shapes. They were like jellyfish, and stuck to him and pulled him away from her.

Lisa heard the voice again, "Stop what you are doing, or I will kill you." She tried to keep her head above water, but she couldn't move her hands, because of the black things pulling her down.

WORD LIST

- remaining　形 残っている
- slip　動 滑る
- as .....　接 .....の時
- try to V　熟 V しようと試みる
- lose one's balance　熟 バランスを崩す
  lose - lost - lost
- pond　名 池
- like ~　前 ~のような
- jellyfish　名 クラゲ
- stick to ~　熟 ~にくっ付く
  stick - stuck - stuck
- pull ~ away　熟 ~を引き離す
- pull ~ down　熟 ~を引き降ろす

LISA
Pine Pond

Ken saw Lisa go underwater. As he searched desperately for her, the only thing he could see was a thin stream of bubbles rising to the surface.

To be continued

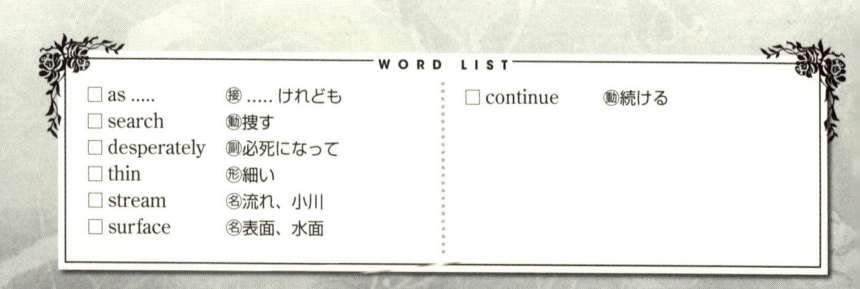

WORD LIST

- as ..... 接 ..... けれども
- search 動 捜す
- desperately 副 必死になって
- thin 形 細い
- stream 名 流れ、小川
- surface 名 表面、水面
- continue 動 続ける

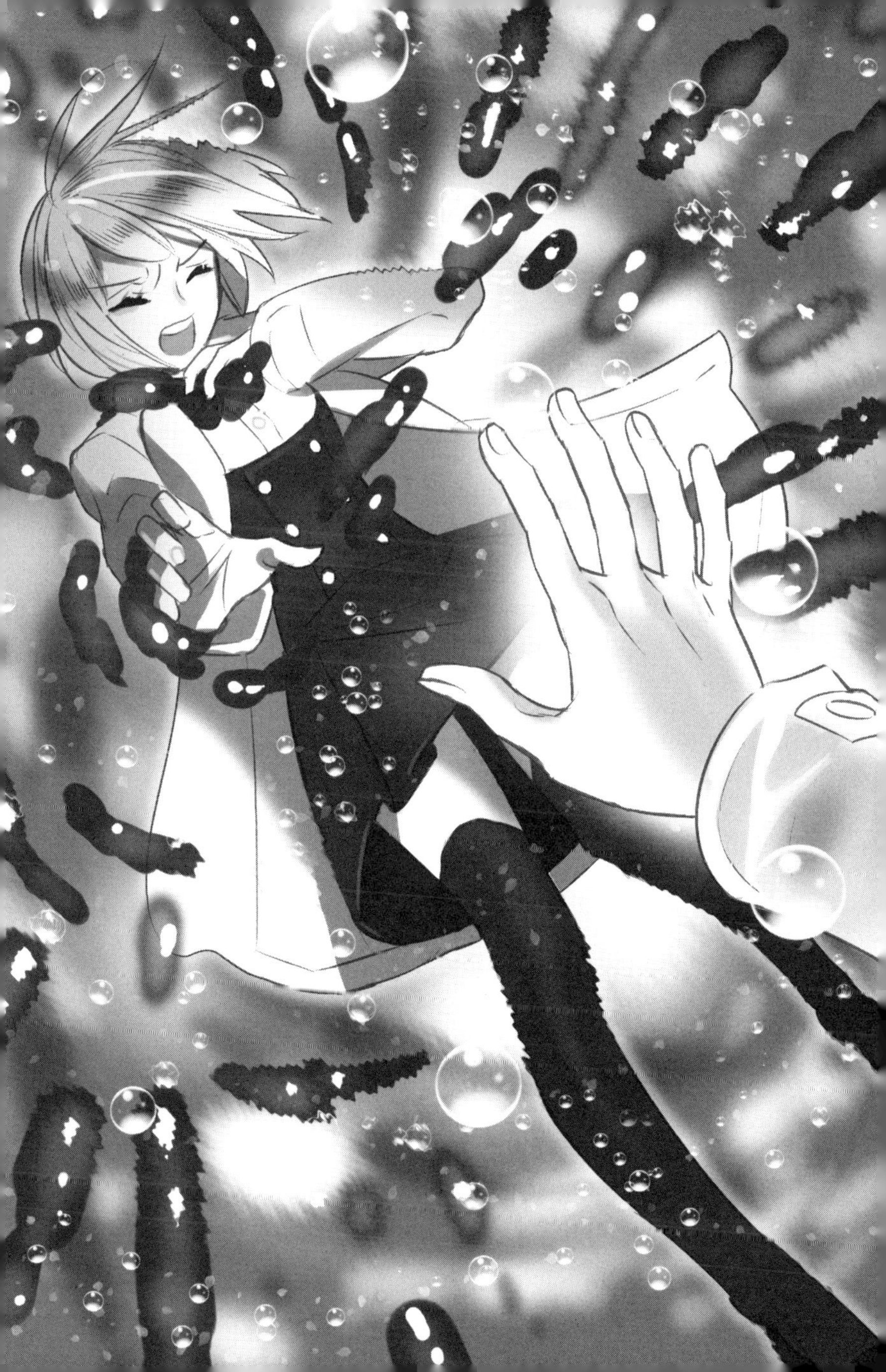

LISA
the Teenage Channeler

Chapter 8
The Milky Way

The Milky Way

Lisa was sinking deeper under the water.

"Who are you? Why are you doing this?" Lisa said in her mind, and the voice answered.

"You are getting in my way. I collect lost spirits. I have them work for me."

"Who are you? Why are you doing this?" Lisa asked.

"I'm a demon. My job is to turn this world into a

WORD LIST

- the Milky Way 熟 天の川
- sink 動 沈む
  sink - sank - sunk(sunken)
- get in one's way 熟 ～の邪魔になる
- lost 形 失われた、道に迷った
- spirit 名 霊、魂
- demon 名 悪魔
- turn A into B 熟 AをBに変える

dark place for demons to live. I collect spirits, and turn them black and evil. You and your boyfriend are in my way. Your mother was also in my way, so I finished her, like I will finish you two now."

"So you're also turning Thomas black?" Lisa asked the demon.

"Haha... Thomas doesn't exist. I pretended to be him to lure you here."

Lisa couldn't think anymore. She was fading into unconsciousness.

--- WORD LIST ---

- evil　形邪悪な
- finish　動終える、殺す
- like .....　接 ..... のように
- exist　動存在する
- pretend　動振りをする
- lure　動おびき出す、誘惑する
- anymore　副もはや、これ以上
- fade　動薄れる、消えていく
- unconsciousness　名無意識

LISA
The Milky Way

"Mother, help me. I have to help the poor spirits. I need to live." Bubbles had almost stopped coming from her mouth, when suddenly she heard her mother's voice.

"Lisa, you have a mission. You can't let him do what he does."

Then a bright light appeared from nowhere and began to cover the whole area. Lisa felt very warm, and felt she was protected by love and kindness.

She heard the devil groan, and his voice finally

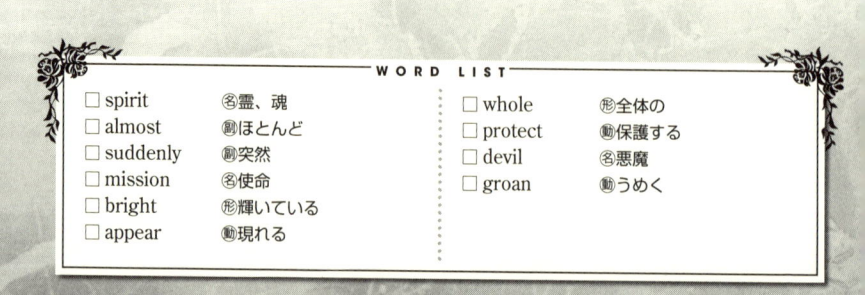

WORD LIST

☐ spirit	名霊、魂	☐ whole	形全体の
☐ almost	副ほとんど	☐ protect	動保護する
☐ suddenly	副突然	☐ devil	名悪魔
☐ mission	名使命	☐ groan	動うめく
☐ bright	形輝いている		
☐ appear	動現れる		

Chapter 8
The Milky Way

disappeared.

Now her body was free and she managed to swim back to the surface, and she could hear Ken's voice.

"Lisa! Lisa!" he was yelling.

Then a miracle happened. She opened her eyes, and she could see.

Ken swam to her and held her. Lisa looked straight into his beautiful brown eyes and said, "I can see. I can see you."

They held each other and kissed. It was their first

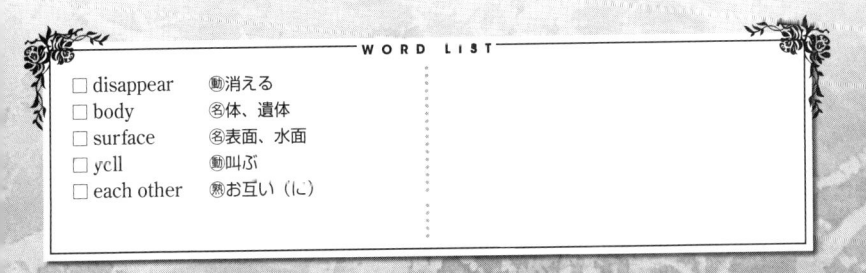

WORD LIST

- disappear　動消える
- body　名体、遺体
- surface　名表面、水面
- yell　動叫ぶ
- each other　熟お互い（に）

kiss.

They began to swim back to the shore. The bright light was now ascending toward the sky, and thousands of small lights from the pond followed it. It looked like the Milky Way. It was the most beautiful sight that they had ever seen.

Lisa said to herself, "Thank you, Mom. I love you."

The End

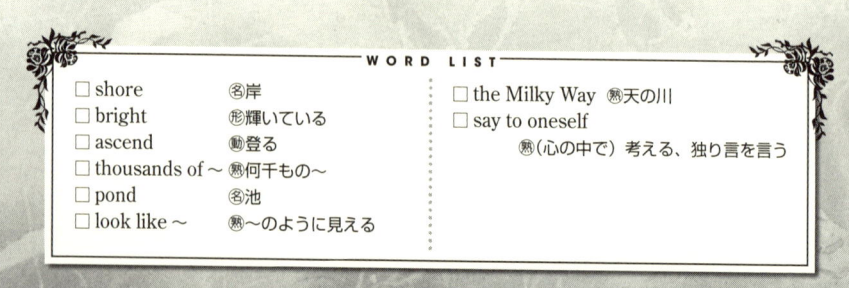

WORD LIST

- shore 名岸
- bright 形輝いている
- ascend 動登る
- thousands of ～ 熟何千もの～
- pond 名池
- look like ～ 熟～のように見える
- the Milky Way 熟天の川
- say to oneself 熟(心の中で) 考える、独り言を言う

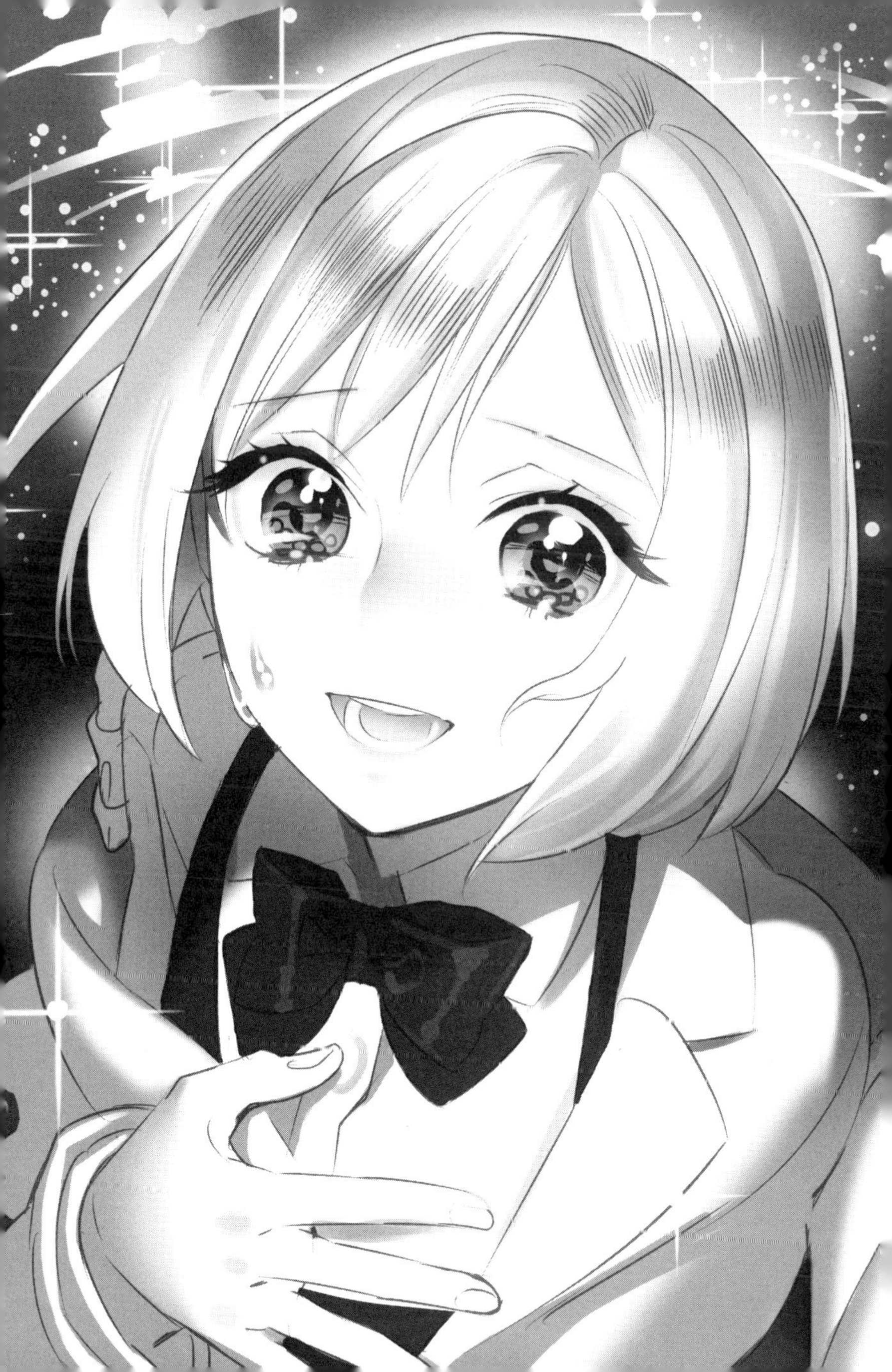

LISA
the Teenage Channeler

Translation

和訳

LISA

和訳

Chapter 1　Lisa's Mission

リサの使命

P.8　9歳の時、リサは交通事故にあった。それ以来、視力を失ってしまった。両親はその事故で亡くなり、彼女は児童養護施設で育てられた。そしてリサはもう17歳になった。

　リサはとても賢く、学校の成績もとても良かった。成績は常にクラストップで、クラスメートからもとても尊敬されていた。しかし、彼女はおとなしく、クラスメートと会話をすることはあまりなかった。

　リサにはずっと黙っていた秘密があった。その事故以来、しばし、死者の声が聞こえるようになったのだ。初め、リサはそれがとても怖かったが、次第に彼らを無視できるようになった。リサは両親の声を聞きたいと思っていたが、両親と話をすることはできなかった。

　リサは両親をとても愛していた。一人っ子だったので、両親もリサの P.10　ことをとても愛していた。母は死の直前に、隣のベッドからリサに語りかけた。「あなたは特別なのよ。使命を忘れないで。」と。リサにはその時、母が意味したことがまだ分からなかった。

　ある晩、リサがベッドに横になっていると、女性の声が聞こえた。「あなただけが私を助けることができるの。あなただけが頼りなの。」リサはいつも通りその声を無視したが、その声はどんどん大きくなった。その女性は同じ言葉を繰り返した。「あなただけが私を助けることができるの。あなただけが頼りなの。」

　リサは眠りにつくことができず、とうとう、その女性に話しかけるのを止めるよう求めた。「もう話しかけないで。私にできることなんてないわ。私は普通の人間なの。他の人に頼んでよ。眠れないじゃない。」

LISA
和訳

　しかし、その声は止むことなく、さらに大きくなった。同じ言葉がこんなにも繰り返されたのは初めてだった。リサは根負けし、「分かったわ。何が望みなの？　手短にね。眠いんだから。」と言った。

　「ほ…、本当に…ありがとう…。私…、ケイ。10年前までここに住んでいたんだけど、雷に打たれて死んだの。」と、その声の主は言った。そして「シスターメアリーに伝えなきゃいけないことがあるので、まだこの世を去れないの。」と続けた。

　リサは興味を持ち、耳を傾け始めた。声の主は「シスターメアリーは母のようだったの。本当によくしてくれた。でも、私はおてんばで、いつも彼女にいたずらばかりしていたの。死ぬ前の日に、私はネックレスを隠したの。ネックレスを見つけられなかった時、彼女はとても慌てて、いたるところを捜し回っていたの。後になって私はそのネックレスは、亡くなったお母さんからのプレゼントだって知ったの。」

　「次の日の放課後、彼女に謝って、どこにネックレスを隠したかを伝えようとしていたの。そこで、あのひどい雷雨でしょ。雨の中を走って帰っている時に、雷に打たれたの。それで、あなたから、ネックレスを隠した場所を彼女に伝えて欲しいの。お願い。」

　リサはケイをとても気の毒だと思い、助けようと決めた。

　ケイはネックレスは地下室の使われていない暖炉の中にあるとリサに伝え、リサは翌朝シスターメアリーにそれを伝えると約束した。「本当にありがとう。やっとこの世を去ることができる。」ケイはそう言い残して消えた。

　翌朝、リサはシスターメアリーのもとへ行き、彼女にその話を伝えた。シスターメアリーは暖炉の中でネックレスを見つけることができた。彼女はリサの目をじっと見つめた。その目には涙が浮かんでいた。

　「さぁ、リリ、自分が何をすべきか分かったわね。あなたは特別なのよ。

LISA
和訳

あなたには使命があるのよ。」

Chapter 2　Mother's Last message
最後の言葉

P.18　リサの母親サラとシスターメアリーは同じ年に、同じ地区で生まれた。二人は親友だった。サラもまた死者の声を聞く力を持っていた。彼女はそのことを秘密にしていたが、17歳の時メアリーにその能力のことを打ち明けた。

「秘密を打ち明けてくれてありがとう。私はあなたは特別だとずっと思っていたの。その能力を使って何をするつもりなの？」

P.19　サラはどう答えるべきか分からなかった。彼女は死者の声には関わりたくなかったので、常にそれらを無視していたのだ。

「神様があなたにその能力を授けたのはきっと理由があるのよ。自分ではどうすることもできない死者たちを助けるべきだと思うわ。そういう人たちは、まだこの世に未練が残っていて、この世を去ることができないのかもしれないわ。あなたはそういう人を助けなければならないのよ。」メアリーは強い口調で言った。

その日から、サラは死者たちがこの世を後にする手助けをした。何百P.20 という死者たちの手助けをした。そして死者のメッセージをその家族や友人に届けた。彼女は死者を助けることに大きな喜びを感じ、彼らを助けることは人生の使命になった。

サラはリサの父親となるダンと結婚したが、その能力については秘密にしていた。二人の間には美しい娘が生まれ、リサと名付けられた。サラはリサを抱きかかえていると、どういうわけかサラはリサが同じ能力

を持っているだろうと分かった。リサが十分な年齢になったら、リサの持つ能力と彼女の使命について話をするつもりだった。

ある日、サラに、ひどく奇妙で恐ろしい声が聞こえ始めた。「止めるのだ。さもないと殺す。」それは男性の声で、ほぼ毎晩、何週間も繰り返された。サラはその声にひどく怯え、しっかり睡眠をとることができず、とても疲れていた。

ある朝、サラはリサとダンを乗せて運転していた。カーブに差し掛かった時、彼女は突然めまいを感じ、意識を失った。車はフェンスを突き破りひっくり返った。救急車が到着し、3人は病院へと運ばれた。ダンは即死だった。サラとリサは重傷だった。次の日の朝、リサは少し回復したが、サラは悪化していた。

医師はサラに「本当に申し上げにくいのですが、もう長くは生きられません。最後に一度娘さんに会いたいですか？」と尋ねた。サラが「ええ。」と答えると、看護師は彼女のベッドを押しリサの隣へ運んだ。死の直前、彼女はリサにメッセージを伝えた。「あなたは特別なの。あなたには使命があるのよ。」彼女はそれ以上言葉を発することができなかった。彼女の呼吸は止まってしまった。

Chapter 3　The Voice from the Well

井戸の少年

リサの目は光を失っていたが、とても美しかった。男の子たちはリサをよくデートに誘ったが、彼女はいつも断っていた。彼女はいつも児童養護施設にまっすぐ帰り、シスターメアリーとお茶を飲みながら話をした。

LISA
和訳

　シスターメアリーに自分の能力について話してからは、二人はよくリサの母親サラについて話した。サラが死者を助けるためにしたことや、どのようにリサが死者の手助けをすることができるのかについて話した。

　ある晩、リサは「助けて。」という声を聞いた。小さな男の子の声で、その声は反響していた。リサはその子に「私に何をして欲しいの？　あなたはどこにいるの？」と尋ねた。

　「僕はデイビッド。森の井戸の中。一人でここに来たんだ。この井戸を見つけて落ちたの。誰も助けてくれないんだ。だからまだここにいるんだ。暗くて寒いよ。ママに僕はここにいるって知らせて。ママに会いたいよ。」彼は泣き始めた。

　リサは、彼は自分が死んでいることに気付いていないのだと分かった。「分かったわ。もう少しだけ待っていて。明日の朝、お母さんにあなたがどこにいるか伝えてあげるから。井戸はどこなの。それとお母さんの名前は？」

　次の日の朝、リサはシスターメアリーに、インターネットで行方不明の男の子を捜すようにお願いした。そしてデイビッドという名前の男の子が一年前から行方不明だと分かった。母親のキャロラインは町の反対側に住んでいた。シスターメアリーはリサを彼女の家まで乗せて行った。

　キャロラインがリサを見た時、なぜ10代の女の子が訪ねて来るのか分からなかったが、シスターメアリーを見て、この二人は聖書を売りに来たのだと思った。「私たちは息子さんのデイビッドについてお話するためにここに来ました。」とリサが言うと、キャロラインは二人を中に通し、お茶を入れてくれた。

　リサはキャロラインにデイビッドの声についての話をした。キャロラインは取り乱した。彼女は息子が死んでいると信じたがらず、とても腹を立てた。キャロラインは二人に出て行くよう求めた。リサはとても悲

LISA
和訳

しかった。リサはただデイビッドの母親を助けようとしただけなのだが、何とも冷たい反応が返って来てしまったのだ。リサは泣き始めた。

「リサ、そんなにがっかりしないで。あなたは正しいことをしているのよ。これは神様があなたに与えた使命なの。あなたはメッセージを伝え続けなければならないの。あなただからできることなのよ。あなたは本当に特別なのよ。」

その日の午後遅く、キャロラインはリサの話について考えていた。ついに、彼女は警察に電話し、森の井戸を捜してもらう決心をした。警察はデイビッドの遺体をその井戸の中で見つけた。

その晩、リサは何もする気になれず、ベッドに横になっていた。彼女はとても悲しかった。「お母さん、どうして私はこんなことをしなければならないの？ 死者のメッセージを伝える使命はそんなにも大切なことなの？」とつぶやいた。

突然、リサはシスターメアリーが下で自分のことを呼んでいるのを聞いた。シスターはお客さんが来ていると言った。キャロラインだった。「今朝は怒ってしまって、本当にごめんなさい。あなたは正しかったわ。警察がデイビッドの体を井戸の中で見つけたの。疑ってしまって本当にごめんなさい。」とキャロラインは目に涙を浮かべながら言った。「あなたには、まだデイビッドの声が聞こえるの？ 彼はここにいるの？」

「彼はあなたの隣にいるし、あなたの声も聞こえているわ。自分が死んでいることを教えてあげて。彼は前に進まないと。」とリサは言った。

「デイビッド、ママはあなたをもう一度抱きしめたいの。でもできないのよ。ママとあなたは、今は違う世界にいるの。いつか、ママもあなたに会いに行くわ。その時まで、さようならなの。おばあちゃんに、よろしく伝えてね。ママがいつもあなたのことを愛してるって忘れないでね。」

LISA

和訳

　リサは「ママ、大好きだよ。じゃあね。」と言うデイビッドの声を聞いた。

Chapter 4　Time Travel

タイムトラベル

P.36
　その年の冬はとても寒かった。例年よりも雪がたくさん降り、児童養護施設の子供たちは庭で雪遊びができてとても喜んでいた。

　リサはキッチンのテーブルでシスターメアリーがお茶を入れてくれるのを待っていた。「今日は、インドの特別なハーブティーを入れたわ。健康に良いハーブがたくさん入っているのよ。飲んでみて。」とシスターメアリーは言った。

P.37
　そのお茶を飲むと、リサはめまいがし始め、眠ってしまった。そして夢を見始めた。その夢はとてもリアルで、夢の中では彼女には視力があった。リサはビーチにいた。目の前には同級生のエミリーが立っていた。

　「こんにちは、エミリー。こんなところで会うなんて思わなかったわ。元気？」リサは尋ねたが、エミリーにはリサの声は聞こえていなかったし、リサのことが見えてもいなかった。リサはエミリーにとっては見えない存在だったのだ。エミリーは紙を砂の上に置き、石の重しを乗せ、前へと歩き出し、そのまま海へ入って行った。とうとう波が彼女を飲み込んでしまい、リサにはもはや彼女のことが見えなくなった。

P.38
　リサはその紙に書かれていることを読んだ。そこには「私はお金を盗んでいません。私はみんなのことが嫌いで、みんなも私のことが嫌いです。誰も私を信じてくれませんでした。もうこれ以上生きていたくありません。」とあった。リサは歩いて町に戻り、そして新聞で6か月先の

LISA
和訳

未来の映像を見ているのだと分かった。

リサには、なぜエミリーが死ななければならないのか分からなかったし、エミリーがお金を盗んだなんて信じられなかった。「彼女がそんなことをしたはずないわ。とてもいい人で正直だもの。」とリサは心の中で思った。すると、まためまいがして、突然シスターメアリーのいるテーブルで意識を取り戻した。

リサはとても長い時間意識が遠のいていたように感じたが、シスターメアリーはリサが眠っていることに気付かなかったと言った。二人は、インドのハーブティーにはリサを未来へ送る力があるのだと分かった。リサはそのお茶をもう一度飲んだが、今回はほんの少しだけにしておいた。再びめまいがして、目を開けると、春だった。

リサは朝の教室にいた。女の子たちが話していた。ある女の子が「クラス旅行のお金がどこに保管されているか知ってる？ 先生のオフィスなのよ。その机の引き出しの中なの。でね、オフィスと引き出しには鍵がかかってないのよ。」と言った。

すると、別の子が、「でも、捕まっちゃうかもしれないよ。グリーン先生はまず私たちを疑うだろうし。」と言った。

「そしたら、グリーン先生が誰か他の人を疑うように仕向ければ良いのよ。例えばエミリーとか。あの子あまりしゃべらないし、それに貧乏でしょ。誰も疑わないわよ。」とまた別の子が言った。

お昼休みの間に彼女たちはそのお金を盗み、少しのお札と封筒をこっそりエミリーのカバンに入れておいた。

グリーン先生は激怒し、クラスの生徒に、クラス旅行のお金について尋ねた。誰も答えなかったので、先生はみんなにカバンを机の上に置くように求めた。そして、エミリーのバッグに封筒とお札を見つけた。グリーン先生はエミリーに残りのお金はどこかと尋ねたが、エミリーはた

LISA
和訳

だ泣くだけだった。

P.42　リサは未来から現実に戻って来ると、シスターメアリーと何ができるかについて話し合った。二人は、一番良いのはグリーン先生にオフィスのドアと机の引き出しに鍵を付けてもらうことだと思った。

　ある日の放課後、リサはこっそりとグリーン先生のオフィスに入り込み、引き出しの中のものを取り出し、机の上に置いておいた。いくつか家具も動かした。次の日、教室でグリーン先生は生徒にその事件について何か知っているか尋ねた。リサが手を上げて発言した。「外から入って来た泥棒の仕業かもしれません。先生、オフィスのドアと引き出しに鍵を付けた方が良いと思います。鍵がないのは危険過ぎます。」

P.43

　グリーン先生は普段はおとなしい女の子がみんなの前で意見を言ったことにとても驚いたが、疑うことなく、リサの提案を真摯に受け止めた。そしてオフィスには鍵が取り付けられた。

　あのインドのハーブティーを飲んで、次に再びリサがビーチを訪れると、エミリーがお母さんと一緒に歩いているのが見えた。二人とも微笑み合っていて、とても幸せそうだった。二人は美しい夕日を眺めていた。リサは太陽が水平線の向こう側へ沈んで行くのを、二人の横で眺めていた。

P.44

Chapter 5　Murderer in Disguise

殺人鬼

P.48　化学のベン・ガーナー先生は40代だったが、ずっと若く見えた。授業はとても面白く、生徒の間でもとても人気があった。リサもその先生のことが好きだったが、それは授業が面白いからではなく、先生の声が

LISA
和訳

死んでしまったお父さんに似ているからだった。

　お父さんは生きていた時、寝る前によくお話をしてくれた。ベンのクラスにいるとリサはお父さんの話を聞いているような感じがした。授業中、リサはよくお父さんの顔を思い描いていた。お父さんが戻って来て、彼女に話しかけてくれているようだった。

　リサは質問するために時々ベン先生のオフィスを訪ねたが、それは授業が分からなかったからではなく、単に先生と話したかったからだった。

　ある日の午後、先生はリサに「もし、とても科学に興味があるのなら、先生の家にあるプロが使う機器を試してみたらいいよ。心配ないよ。学校はもう終わったし、午後は何もやることがないから。家に来てみないかい？」と尋ねた。

　「シスターメアリーに電話して、大丈夫か聞いてみないと。」とリサは言った。

　「大丈夫だよ。5時までには家に送るから。わざわざシスターに電話する必要はないよ。」

　リサはうなずき、ベンの古い車に乗り込み、彼の家へと向かった。リサはお父さんと一緒に車に乗っているように感じ、二人は多くの会話を楽しんだ。会話が途切れた時、リサには女の子の声が聞こえた。

　「逃げて！　死ぬ気で逃げて！　逃げて！　本当に死ぬ気で逃げて！この男は危険なの！」

　リサはどうすべきか分からなかった。ベンと一緒に車の中にいるという状況に置かれていた。ベンが隣にいたので、リサは声の主に何も尋ねることができなかった。その声は止まることなく、同じ言葉を繰り返し続けた。リサは恐ろしくなった。

　二人はベンの家につき、ベンはリサをリビングルームのテーブルに座らせた。「お茶を入れるね。」と言い、ベンはキッチンへ向かった。例の

LISA
和訳

声はまだそこにいたので、リサは声を潜めて尋ねた。「どういうことなの？ 彼って誰なの？」

「あぁ、やった。聞こえるのね。逃げて。彼は殺人鬼よ。」とその声は言った。

「殺人鬼？ 誰のことを言ってるの？」リサは尋ねた。

「あの男よ。ベン・ガーナー。あいつは私を殺したの。あいつはお茶の中に何かを入れて、私は眠くなって、そして、あいつは…。」声の主は泣き始めた。「あいつは私を殺した後、化学薬品で私の死体を溶かし、骨を裏庭に埋めたのよ。逃げて。命がけで。お茶を飲んじゃダメよ。」その声は警告した。

リサは自分が聞いたことが信じられなかったが、とにかく誰かに助けを求めなければと思った。

ベンがお茶を持って部屋に戻り、テーブルについた。リサはトイレを借りたいと伝え、携帯電話をポケットに忍ばせながらトイレへ向かった。できるだけ平静を装いながら。

リサはトイレでシスターメアリーに、警察に電話をして、警官をベンの家までよこして欲しいというボイスメールを送った。

リサはテーブルに戻り、お茶を飲まずにできるだけ長く話した。

「どうしてお茶を飲まないんだい？ 美味しいのに。」とベンは言った。もうお茶を飲むしかなかった。ほんの少しだけ飲み、「あっ…ごめんなさい、ガーナー先生、このお茶、私には少し濃過ぎるみたい。もう少し薄めてもらえますか？」と言った。これは時間稼ぎだったが、既に飲んだお茶のせいで眠くなり、とうとう眠ってしまった。

ベンはハサミを持って戻って来ると、リサの後ろ髪をまとめて切り、それをボトルに入れた。そして、リサをロープで椅子にしばりつけた。

リサが目を覚ますと、ベンが彼女のちょうど横で呼吸しているのが聞

こえた。手にはナイフを持っていた。

あの女の子は「起きて！ 起きてよ！」と叫んでいた。

「お母さん、助けて。まだ死にたくないの。」リサはつぶやいた。

ベンがナイフを振りかざしたその時、リサは銃声とベンの叫び声を聞いた。銃弾が窓を突き破りベンの肩に当たったのだ。ベンは床に倒れた。数名の警官がドアから家の中に入って来て、リサのもとへ駆けつけ彼女のロープをほどいた。ベンは逮捕された。

「彼は別の女の子を殺したかもしれないわ。」とリサは警官に伝えた。警官は家の中を捜し、髪の毛が入っている別のボトルを見つけ、その後、裏庭に埋められた女の子の骨も発見した。

DNA鑑定の後、女の子の名前はアデリン・ブラウンで、一年間も行方不明になっていたことが分かった。アデリンが姿を消した時、彼女は17歳だった。

リサはアデリンのお墓に花を供えに行った。お礼を言いたかったが、もはやアデリンの声は聞こえなかった。リサはアデリンがやっと安心して、旅立ったのだと思った。

Chapter 6　Ken's Secret

ケンの秘密

ケン・ブラックは18歳。とてもハンサムで成績も非常に優秀だった。たくさんの女の子たちが彼と話したがったが、女の子にはあまり興味がなさそうだった。

ケンには恥ずべき秘密があった。10歳の時、わけもなく死体が見たくなったのだ。そこで、こっそり墓地に行き、新しいお墓を見つけ、棺

LISA
和訳

桶を見つけるまで掘り返した。そして棺桶のふたをたたき割り、同年代の女の子の顔を見た。そして、彼は怖くなり逃げ出してしまった。

それ以来、彼はどこに行っても女の子の幽霊を見るようになった。彼はひどい罪の意識を感じ、何度か自殺をしようとさえした。ケンは、そんな悪いことをしたと誰にも知られたくなかったので、その秘密を誰にも言えなかった。その女の子の幽霊は彼に話しかけているようだったが、聞こえなかった。その子は怒っていると思ったので、ケンは無視していた。

ある日、リサが校庭のベンチに座っていると、女の子の声が聞こえた。その子は誰かに話しかけているようだった。「お父さんを助けて。私が死んでから、お酒をたくさん飲むようになってしまったの。そして、仕事も家も失ってしまって、今は路上で生活しているの。」その子は、明らかに、リサに話しかけているのではなく、その代わりに、リサの隣に座っているケンに話しかけていた。

「お父さんは、私が死んだのは自分のせいだと思っているの。私がお父さんにアイスクリームを買って来てって頼んだから、私を一人家に残して出かけて行ったの。その時だったの、あのひどい男が入って来て、私を殺したの。お父さんのせいじゃないのよ。マークっていう名前の男が私を殺したの。強盗じゃないの。彼はお母さんの愛人なの。私を殺したのはマークよ。」その子は続けた。

リサは何とかしなければと思い、隣に座っているケンに話しかけようと決心した。

「ねぇ、ごめんなさい。あの子が言っていること聞こえる？」と、リサがケンに尋ねると、ケンはひどく驚いた。

「君も彼女が見えるの？」ケンは尋ねた。

「いいえ、目が見えないから。でも聞こえるの。私、リサ・ホワイト。

LISA
和訳

信じられないかもしれないけど、私には死んだ人たちの声が聞こえるの。だから私は彼らが安らげることができるよう手助けをしているの。あなたに見えている幽霊はとても大事なメッセージを伝えているわ。」

「あの子は僕に対して怒っているんじゃないのかい？　何も聞こえないんだ。見えるだけなんだ。ずっと僕にとりついてるんだ。たぶん僕が悪いんだけど。」

「でも、とにかく、彼女を助けるべきだと思うわ。もし、あなたが聞こえないなら、私が助けになるから。彼女は怒ってないみたいよ。彼女に何をしたの？」

「小さい頃に、悪いことをね。いずれにせよ、もし彼女を助けられるなら、助けたいよ。手を貸してくれるかい？」

リサはその幽霊に、ケンには声が聞こえていないことと、自分がケンにメッセージを伝えると言った。すると、幽霊はリサに話をし始めた。

「お母さんは浮気をしていたの。私はあまりお母さんと仲良くなかったし、お母さんも私を嫌っていたの。お母さんの愛人のマークも私とお父さんを嫌っていたの。マークはお母さんを自分のものにするために私たちを殺したいと思っていたの。でも、お父さんが出ていたから、その日に殺されたのは私だけだったんだけど。警察は手がかりを見つけることができなかったわ。強盗の仕業だって…。」女の子は泣き始めた。

ケンとリサは図書館に行き、ケンがインターネットで調べてみた。すると、8年前に殺された女の子はエリカ・テルフォードだと分かった。殺された時、彼女は10歳だった。

二人はエリカの父親を捜すため、街へ出かけ、現在路上で生活しているフランク・テルフォードを見つけた。長いあごひげが生えていて、片手にはウイスキーのボトルを持っていた。とても不健康そうだった。

二人がまさに話しかけようとした時、彼は突然うめき声をあげた。手

LISA
和訳

で胸を押さえ、倒れ込んだ。二人は救急車を呼んだが、遅過ぎた。心臓は止まっていた。

ケンはフランクの霊がその体から離れて行くのを見た。そして、フランクの霊は何が起きたのか分からず、あたりを見回していた。そして、自分の方に走って来るエリカに目を向けた。エリカはお父さんの腕に飛び込み、彼を抱きしめた。エリカとフランクは互いに微笑み合い、消えてしまった。

その日、時間が経ってからリサとケンは殺人鬼のマークに対して何をすべきか話していた。二人はその殺人鬼を見つけ出すためにできることは全てした。二人は何日間か捜し続けたが、とうとうマーク・ボルドウィンという地元で中古車の販売員をしている男を見つけた。

ケンと一緒に時間を過ごせば過ごすほど、リサはケンに惹かれていった。ケンはとても優しく、いつもリサの気持ちを考えてくれた。リサが男の人に好意を寄せたのは初めてだった。ケンもリサに対して同じ気持ちを抱いていた。ケンは彼女の手を引くのが好きだったし、ずっとこんな風に助けてあげられたらと思った。

リサとケンは中古車を展示している駐車場へ行き、マークがどんな人か確かめようと決心した。ケンの車で二人がそこについた時、数台のパトカーが店の前に止まっていた。二人は警官に何があったのか尋ねたが、女性が殺されたということが分かった。

亡くなった女性はエリカの母親だと後々分かった。警察は愛人のマークに疑いをかけ、逮捕した。彼はエリカの殺害を含め、数件の殺人について白状した。

「人はどうしてこんな風に憎み合い、殺し合うの? どうして人間は優しくなれないの? どうして神様は世の中をこんな風に作ったの? 何のために私はこんなことをしているの?」リサは泣き始めた。

ケンは彼女に手を回して「リサ、大丈夫だよ。リサは正しいことをしているんだよ。リサが助けた人はみんな、愛で満たされてこの世を去って行ったんだよ。でも、もう一人でそうする必要はないよ。僕がいつも一緒にいるから。」と言った。

　そして腕の中にリサを抱き寄せた。

Chapter 7　Pine Pond

黒い影

　リサとケンは互いに助け合い始めた。ケンには幽霊が見え、リサは彼らの声を聞くことができた。リサとケンは互いに恋に落ち始めた。二人は完ぺきなチームだった。

　二人は共に、たくさんの魂が安らぎを見つけ、この世を去ることができるよう手助けをした。ケンは最初、単にリサを助けたくて始めたのだが、しばらくすると、彼は世界をより良い場所にするため、とても大事なことをしていると感じるようになった。

　ある日の午後、リサがケンと歩いていると、子供の声が聞こえた。「助けて。水の中にいるの。ボートから落ちておぼれたの。誰も見つけてくれないんだ。パイン池に来て僕を見つけて。」

　リサは男の子に名前を尋ねた。名前はトーマスだった。リサとケンはインターネットでその男の子を捜したが、その子についての情報は何一つ見つけられなかった。

　パイン池は町の外れにあった。週末はボートや魚釣りを楽しむ人がいる場所だった。

　次の日の午後、二人はケンの車で池へ向かった。水曜日だったので、

LISA
和訳

あまり多くの人はいなかった。彼らはボート小屋の前に車を止め、桟橋へと歩き始めた。

桟橋に立って、リサはトーマスに呼びかけた。「助けに来て。助けに来て。」という声だけが聞こえた。彼はとても弱っているようだった。

「池の表面に何か見える？」ケンに尋ねたが、ケンは何も見えないと言った。

二人はボートを借りて、男の子がいる場所が分かるかどうか池を回ってみようと決めた。

「君は来ない方がいいよ。危ないかもしれないから。もし何か起きたら、僕は岸まで泳いで戻れるけど、君は…。」ケンが言った。

「一緒に行くわ。あなたは声を聞けないから私が必要でしょ。それにあなたと一緒にいるんだから私は大丈夫でしょ。しっかりしてね。一緒に行かせて。」とリサは強く言った。

二人はボートに乗り込み、池の中心へと向かってこいで行った。リサは男の子をもう一度呼んでみたが、今度は違う声が聞こえた。

それは男の声で「止めるんだ。さもないと殺すぞ。」と言うのだった。ボートが突然揺れ始め、リサとケンはボートのへりにしがみついた。一つのオールは流され、沈んでしまい、水はボートの中にも入って来た。

ケンはボートが黒い影に囲まれているのが分かった。それらは小さな動物のようだった。何百という数がいた。

ケンはリサの手をしっかり握ろうとした。リサは残っていたオールが滑り落ちて行くのを感じた。リサはそれをつかもうとした時、バランスを崩し、池の中に落ちてしまった。

ケンにはその黒い物体がリサを取り囲んでいるのが見えた。そして彼はリサを救うため水に飛び込んだ。彼もまた黒い物体に囲まれた。それらはまるでクラゲのようで、彼にまとわりつき、リサから引き離した。

LISA
和訳

　リサは「止めるんだ。さもないと殺すぞ。」という声をもう一度聞いた。リサは頭を水の外へ出そうとしたが、黒い物体が彼女を引っ張るので手を動かすことができなかった。

　ケンはリサが沈んで行くのを見た。彼はリサを必死で捜したが、見えたのは水面に昇って来る細い泡の流れだけだった。

Chapter 8　The Milky Way

天の川

　リサは深く沈んでいた。「誰なの？　何でこんなことをするの？」リサが心の中で叫ぶと、声の主は答えた。「お前は邪魔なんだ。俺はさまよっている魂を集めている。そいつらを俺のために働かせるんだ。」

　「誰なの？　何でこんなことをするのよ？」リサは尋ねた。

　「悪魔だよ。俺の仕事はこの世を悪魔が住む暗い場所に変えることだ。魂を集めて、それを黒く、悪に染めるんだ。お前と彼氏が邪魔なんだよ。お前の母親も邪魔だったから殺したんだ、今、二人を殺そうとしているようにな。」

　「それじゃ、トーマスも悪に染めてるの？」リサは悪魔に尋ねた。

　「ははっ。トーマスなんて存在しない。俺がお前をここにおびき出すため、トーマスの振りをしたんだ。」

　リサはそれ以上考えることができなかった。意識が遠のいていた。「お母さん、助けて。かわいそうな魂たちを助けなくちゃならないの。生きなくちゃいけないの。」もうリサの口からは泡が出て来なくなった。そして、その時突然、リサはお母さんの声を聞いた。

　「リサ、あなたには使命があるのよ。悪魔の思い通りにさせちゃダメ。」

111

LISA
和訳

　すると、まばゆいばかりの光がどこからともなく現れて、池全体を覆い始めた。リサはとても温かく、愛と優しさで守られていると感じた。

　悪魔のうなり声が聞こえ、ついには悪魔の声も消えた。

　体が自由になり何とか水面に上がって来ることができ、ケンの声が聞こえた。

　「リサ！　リサ！」ケンは叫んでいた。

　そして、奇跡が起こった。リサが目を開けると、目が見えるようになっていたのだ。

　ケンが泳いで来て、彼女を抱きしめた。そしてリサは彼の美しい茶色の目をまっすぐ見つめ言った。「見える。あなたのことが見えるわ。」

　二人は抱き合いキスをした。それが初めてのキスだった。

　二人は岸へと泳ぎ始めた。そのまばゆい光は空へと昇って行き、池からの数千もの小さな光がそれに続いた。それはまるで天の川のようであった。彼らがそれまでに見た中で一番美しい光景だった。

　リサはつぶやいた。「ありがとう。ママ。愛してるわ。」

【完】

LISA
the Teenage Channeler

Index

索引

☐ a **little** bit	[lítl]	熟	28, 39, 54
☐ a lock of **hair**	[héər]	熟	55
☐ a **lot**	[lát]	熟	64
☐ a lot more than **usual**	[júːʒuəl]	熟	36
☐ a **lot of** ~	[lát]	熟	50, 76
☐ a pair of **scissors**	[sízərz]	熟	55
☐ **ability**	[əbíləti]	名	18, 20, 26
☐ **accident**	[æksədənt]	名	8
☐ **alive**	[əláiv]	形	48
☐ **almost**	[ɔ́ːlmoust]	副	21, 88
☐ **alone**	[əlóun]	副	27, 64, 73
☐ **ambulance**	[æmbjuləns]	名	21, 69
☐ and **so**	[sóu]	熟	67
☐ **anymore**, any more	[ènimɔ́ːr]	副熟	11, 22, 38, 58, 73, 87
☐ **anyway**	[éniwèi]	副	53, 66
☐ **apologize**	[əpálədʒàiz]	動	13
☐ **appear**	[əpíər]	動	88
☐ **arrest**	[ərést]	動	57, 72
☐ **as ....**	[əz]	接	73, 81, 82
☐ as **always**	[ɔ́ːlweiz]	熟	10
☐ as **normal** as possible	[nɔ́ːrməl]	熟	54
☐ **ascend**	[əsénd]	動	90
☐ **ask** ~ out on a **date**	[déit]	熟	26
☐ at **first**	[fɔ́ːrst]	熟	9, 76
☐ **away**	[əwéi]	副	39
☐ **basement**	[béismənt]	名	13
☐ be **about** to V	[əbáut]	熟	68
☐ be hit by **lightning**	[láitniŋ]	熟	11, 13
☐ be seriously **injured**	[índʒərd]	熟	22
☐ be **surrounded** by ~	[səráundid]	熟	80
☐ be **trapped** in ~	[trǽpt]	熟	51
☐ **beard**	[bíərd]	名	68
☐ bedtime **story**	[stɔ́ːri]	熟	48
☐ **Bible**	[báibl]	名	29
☐ **bill**	[bíl]	名	41
☐ **blind**	[bláind]	形	8, 26, 65
☐ **body**	[bádi]	名	30, 53, 62, 69, 89
☐ **bother**	[báðər]	動	50
☐ **break** into ~	[bréik]	熟	57
☐ break **open** ~	[óupən]	熟	62
☐ **breathe**	[bríːð]	動	22, 55
☐ **bright**	[bráit]	形	88, 90
☐ **bring up** ~	[bríŋ ʌp]	熟	8
☐ **bullet**	[búlit]	名	57
☐ **burglar**	[bɔ́ːrglər]	名	65, 68
☐ **bury**	[béri]	動	53, 58
☐ **buy** time	[bái]	熟	55
☐ **call** the police	[kɔ́ːl]	熟	30, 54
☐ **chemical**	[kémikəl]	名	53
☐ **chemistry**	[kéməstri]	名	48
☐ **clearly**	[klíərli]	副	64
☐ **close** to ~	[klóus]	熟	67
☐ **clue**	[klúː]	名	67
☐ **coffin**	[kɔ́fin]	名	62
☐ come **through** ~	[θrúː]	熟	57
☐ commit **suicide**	[kəmit súːəsàid]	熟	63
☐ **communicate** with ~	[kəmjúːnəkèit]	熟	9
☐ **confess** to ~	[kənfés]	熟	72
☐ **considerate**	[kənsídərət]	形	71
☐ **continue**	[kəntínjuː]	動	12, 14, 22, 32, 44, 58, 65, 71, 73, 82
☐ **conversation**	[kà:nvərséiʃən]	名	51
☐ **create**	[kriéit]	動	73
☐ **cry**	[krái]	動	27, 30, 42, 53, 68, 73
☐ cry **out**	[áut]	熟	57
☐ **curious**	[kjúəriəs]	形	12
☐ **curve**	[kɔ́ːrv]	名	21
☐ **dangerous**	[déindʒərəs]	形	43, 51, 79
☐ **decide** to V	[disáid]	熟	11, 13, 30, 65, 71, 78

Word	Pronunciation	Part	Pages
deliver	[dilívər]	動	19, 22, 30
demon	[díːmən]	名	86
desperately	[déspərətli]	副	82
devil	[dévəl]	名	88
die immediately	[imíːdiətli]	熟	22
different	[dífərənt]	形	32, 80
disappear	[disəpíər]	動	58, 69, 89
disguise	[disgáiz]	名	48
dissolve	[dizálv]	動	53
do well in school	[skúːl]	熟	8, 62
doubt	[dáut]	動	31, 41
downstairs	[dáunstéərz]	名	31
drawer	[drɔ́ːr]	名	40, 42
drown	[dráun]	動	77
drowsy	[dráuzi]	形	55
dug	[dʌ́g]	動	62
each other	[íːtʃ ʌ́ðər]	熟	44, 69, 72, 76, 89
echo	[ékou]	動	27
else	[éls]	副	11, 40, 64
embrace	[imbréis]	動	69
enjoy boating and fishing	[indʒɔ́i]	熟	77
enough	[inʌ́f]	副	20
envelope	[énvəlòup]	名	41
equipment	[ikwípmənt]	名	49
everywhere	[évrihwèər]	副	12, 63
evil	[íːvəl]	形	87
exist	[igzíst]	動	87
fade	[féid]	動	87
fall asleep	[əslíːp]	熟	37, 39, 53, 55
fall down	[fɔ́ːl]	熟	69
fall off ~	[ɔ́ːf]	熟	80
fault	[fɔ́ːlt]	名	64, 66
feel dizzy	[dízi]	熟	21, 37, 39
feel guilty	[gílti]	熟	63
feel like ~	[fíːl]	熟	48, 50
filled with ~	[fíld]	熟	14, 31, 73
find out that	[fáind]	熟	68
finish	[fíniʃ]	動	87
fireplace	[fáiərplèis]	名	13, 14
for a long time	[lɔ́ːŋ]	熟	39, 66
for no particular reason	[pərtíkjulər]	熟	62
for one's life	[láif]	熟	51, 53
forest	[fɔ́ːrist]	名	27, 30
forget	[fərgét]	動	10, 32
forward	[fɔ́ːrwərd]	副	37
furniture	[fɔ́ːrnitʃər]	名	42
gentle	[dʒéntl]	形	71
get enough sleep	[inʌ́f]	熟	21
get in one's way	[gét]	熟	86
get upset	[ʌpsét]	熟	29
give up	[gív ʌ́p]	熟	11
go back to ~	[bǽk]	熟	26, 54
grave	[gréiv]	名	58, 62
graveyard	[gréivjɑ̀ːrd]	名	62
groan	[gróun]	動	69, 88
haunt	[hɔ́ːnt]	動	66
have an affair	[əféər]	熟	67
head for ~	[héd]	熟	50
help ~ out	[hélp]	熟	76
herb tea	[ɔ́ːrb]	熟	36, 39, 43
hid	[híd]	動	12
hidden	[hídn]	動	13
hope	[hóup]	動	10
hundreds of ~	[hʌ́ndrədz]	熟	19, 80
ignore	[ignɔ́ːr]	動	9, 10, 19, 63
important	[impɔ́ːrtənt]	形	31, 66, 76
in front of ~	[frʌ́nt]	熟	37, 43, 72, 78
in one's forties	[fɔ́ːrtiz]	熟	48

115

☐ incident	[ínsədənt]	名	43
☐ including ~	[inklú:diŋ]	前	72
☐ insist	[insíst]	動	19, 79
☐ install	[instɔ́:l]	動	42
☐ instead	[instéd]	副	64
☐ invisible	[invízabl]	形	37
☐ jellyfish	[dʒélifiʃ]	名	81
☐ keep ~ to oneself	[kí:p]	熟	67
☐ lead ~ by the hand	[lí:d]	熟	71
☐ lid	[líd]	名	63
☐ like	[láik]	接	87
☐ like ~	[láik]	前	12, 40, 49, 71, 73, 81
☐ local	[lóukəl]	形	71
☐ lock	[lák]	名	40, 42
☐ look around	[əráund]	熟	69
☐ look for ~	[lúk]	熟	68
☐ look like ~	[láik]	熟	80, 90
☐ lose one's balance	[bǽləns]	熟	81
☐ lost	[lɔ́:st]	形	86
☐ lot	[lát]	名	71
☐ louder and louder	[láudər]	熟	10
☐ lure	[lúər]	動	87
☐ lying	[láiiŋ]	動	10, 30
☐ make ~ a better place	[pléis]	熟	77
☐ maybe	[méibi]	副	66
☐ meant	[mént]	動	10
☐ missing	[mísiŋ]	形	28, 58
☐ mission	[míʃən]	名	8, 10, 14, 20, 22, 30, 88
☐ mission in life	[láif]	熟	20
☐ move on	[mú:v]	熟	32
☐ murder	[mɔ́:rdər]	名	72
☐ murderer	[mɔ́:rdərər]	名	48, 52, 69
☐ name A B	[néim]	熟	20
☐ neighborhood	[néibərhùd]	名	18
☐ next to ~	[nékst]	熟	10, 22, 51, 65
☐ nod	[nád]	動	50
☐ not ..... have anything to do with ~	[éniθiŋ]	熟	19
☐ notice	[nóutis]	動	39
☐ oar	[ɔ́:r]	名	80
☐ officer	[ɔ́:fisər]	名	54, 57, 72
☐ on the Internet	[íntərnèt]	熟	28, 68
☐ opinion	[əpínjən]	名	43
☐ orphanage	[ɔ́:rfənidʒ]	名	8, 26, 36
☐ over time	[óuvər]	熟	9
☐ park	[pá:rk]	動	72, 78
☐ pass away	[əwéi]	熟	22
☐ pass out	[pǽs]	熟	21
☐ permission	[pərmíʃən]	名	50
☐ pier	[píər]	名	78
☐ play tricks on ~	[tríks]	熟	12
☐ pond	[pánd]	名	76, 78, 81, 90
☐ pretend	[priténd]	動	87
☐ protect	[prətékt]	動	88
☐ pull ~ away	[púl]	熟	81
☐ pull ~ down	[dáun]	熟	81
☐ raise	[réiz]	動	43
☐ reaction	[riǽkʃən]	名	30
☐ realize	[rí:əlàiz]	動	28
☐ remaining	[riméiniŋ]	形	81
☐ rent	[rént]	動	78
☐ respect	[rispékt]	動	8
☐ rest	[rést]	名	41
☐ rim	[rím]	名	80
☐ rock	[rák]	動	80
☐ roll over	[róul]	熟	21
☐ row	[róu]	動	79
☐ run away	[rʌ́n]	熟	63
☐ rush	[rʌ́ʃ]	動	57

☐ say **hi** to ~	[hái]	熟	32
☐ say to oneself	[séi]	熟	31, 57, 90
☐ scared	[skéərd]	形	9, 51, 63
☐ scary	[skéəri]	形	21
☐ science	[sáiəns]	名	49
☐ search	[sə́ːrtʃ]	動	12, 28, 30, 57, 68, 77, 82
☐ secretly	[síːkritli]	副	41, 42, 62
☐ send a **voicemail**	[vɔ́ismèil]	熟	54
☐ seriously	[síəriəsli]	副	43
☐ shameful	[ʃéimfəl]	形	62
☐ shore	[ʃɔ́ːr]	名	79, 90
☐ since ~	[síns]	前	8
☐ sink	[síŋk]	動	44, 86
☐ slip	[slíp]	動	81
☐ smart	[smɑ́ːrt]	形	8
☐ some **pieces** of ~	[píːsiz]	熟	42
☐ **some** time	[sʌ́m]	熟	76
☐ someday	[sʌ́mdèi]	副	32
☐ somehow	[sʌ́mhàu]	副	20
☐ soul	[sóul]	名	69
☐ **sound** like ~	[sáund]	熟	48
☐ sound **weak**	[wíːk]	熟	78
☐ spirit	[spírit]	名	76, 86, 88
☐ steal	[stíːl]	動	38
☐ **stick** to ~	[stík]	熟	81
☐ still	[stíl]	副	10, 19, 27, 31, 52
☐ stream	[stríːm]	名	82
☐ suddenly	[sʌ́dnli]	副	21, 31, 39, 68, 80, 88
☐ suggestion	[səgdʒéstʃən]	名	43
☐ surface	[sə́ːrfis]	名	82, 89
☐ suspect	[səspékt]	動	40, 43, 72
☐ swallow	[swɑ́lou]	動	38
☐ **talk** about ~	[tɔ́ːk]	熟	26, 29, 42, 50, 69
☐ tear	[tíər]	名	14, 31
☐ terrible	[térəbl]	形	13, 64
☐ terrified	[térəfàid]	形	21
☐ the **dead**	[déd]	熟	9, 18, 26, 66, 72
☐ the horizon	[həráizn]	熟	44
☐ the **Milky** Way	[mílki]	熟	86, 90
☐ the police	[pəlíːs]	熟	30, 67, 72
☐ the **present**	[préznt]	熟	42
☐ the **same** ability as ~	[séim]	熟	20
☐ thief	[θíːf]	名	43
☐ thin	[θín]	形	82
☐ **think** to oneself	[θíŋk]	熟	39
☐ **thousands** of ~	[θáuzəndz]	熟	90
☐ thunderstorm	[θʌ́ndərstɔ̀ːrm]	名	13
☐ tie	[tái]	動	55
☐ **too** ~	[túː]	副	43
☐ too **late**	[léit]	熟	69
☐ too **strong** for me	[strɔ́ːŋ]	熟	55
☐ tough	[tʌ́f]	形	79
☐ **track** ~ down	[trǽk]	熟	71
☐ try **out** ~	[áut]	熟	49
☐ try to **cling** on to ~	[klíŋ]	熟	80
☐ try to V	[trái]	熟	29, 54, 63, 69, 81
☐ turn A **into** B	[íntə]	熟	86
☐ **turn** out that	[tə́ːrn]	熟	58, 72
☐ unconsciousness	[ʌnkɑ́nʃəsnəs]	名	87
☐ unused	[ʌnjúːzd]	形	13
☐ upset	[ʌpsét]	形	12
☐ very	[véri]	副	67
☐ vision	[víʒən]	名	38
☐ **wait** for ~	[wéit]	熟	28, 36
☐ warn	[wɔ́ːrn]	動	50
☐ **weigh** ~ down	[wéi]	熟	37
☐ well	[wél]	名	26, 28, 30
☐ whole	[hóul]	形	88
☐ **why** don't you V?	[hwái]	熟	50, 54
☐ yell	[jél]	動	89

117

●大学受験 英文多読シリーズ

霊感少女リサ

発行日:2012年10月29日 初版発行
　　　　2016年11月15日 第7版発行

著　者:安河内哲也
発行者:永瀬昭幸

編集担当:村本悠
発行所:株式会社ナガセ
　　　　〒180-0003　東京都武蔵野市吉祥寺南1-29-2
　　　　出版事業部(東進ブックス)
　　　　TEL:0422-70-7456／FAX:0422-70-7457
　　　　URL:http://www.toshin.com/books/
　　　　(本書を含む東進ブックスの最新情報は上記「WEB書店」をご覧ください)

カバー・本文デザイン:LIGHTNING
イラスト:碧風羽
執筆協力・校閲:Matthew Radich／Mickey Acorn／Nadia McKechnie
翻訳・編集協力:武藤一也／山越友子

DTP:株式会社秀文社
印刷・製本:日経印刷株式会社
音声収録・編集:財団法人 英語教育協議会(ELEC)
音声出演:安河内哲也／Rachel Walzer

※落丁・乱丁本は着払いにて小社出版事業部宛にお送りください。新本にお取り替えいたします。
※本書を無断で複写・複製・転載することを禁じます。

Tetsuya Yasukochi 2012 Printed in Japan
ISBN978-4-89085-553-7　C7382

── 音声ダウンロードサイト ──

http://www.toshin.com/books/
※音声ダウンロードの際は、下記のパスワードが必要です。詳細は上記のサイトをご参照ください。
Password : 2lxU4TG8

東進ブックス

編集部より

この本を読み終えた君に オススメの3冊！

英文多読シリーズ第2弾!! 舞台は東京。親も家も失い、突然ホームレスになったメグ。ある時、謎の男に出会って…!?

ミラクルアイドルメグ第2巻!! いよいよクライマックスへ突入。メグ、ナオミ、モモ…トップアイドルは一体、誰!?

英文多読シリーズ第3弾!! わずか12歳で挫折を味わった少年ダイキ。グレて、ついには暴走族の一員となるが…!?

体験授業

この本を書いた講師の授業を受けてみませんか？

東進では有名実力講師陣の授業を無料で体験できる『体験授業』を行っています。
「わかる」授業、「完璧に」理解できるシステム
そして最後まで「頑張れる」雰囲気を
実際に体験してください。

※1講座(90分×1回)を受講できます。
※お電話でご予約ください。
　連絡先は付録9ページをご覧ください。
※お友達同士でも受講できます。

安河内先生の主な担当講座　※2016年度
「有名大突破！戦略英語解法」など

東進の合格の秘訣が次ページに

合格の秘訣1 全国屈指の実力講師陣

ベストセラー著者の
なんと7割が東進の講師陣!!

東進ハイスクール・
東進衛星予備校では、
そうそうたる講師陣が君を熱く指導する!

　本気で実力をつけたいと思うなら、やはり根本から理解させてくれる一流講師の授業を受けることが大切です。東進の講師は、日本全国から選りすぐられた大学受験のプロフェッショナル。何万人もの受験生を志望校合格へ導いてきたエキスパート達です。

英語

講師	キャッチコピー
安河内 哲也 先生 [英語]	数えきれないほどの受験生の偏差値を改造、難関大へ送り込む!
今井 宏 先生 [英語]	予備校界のカリスマ講師。君に驚きと満足、そして合格を与えてくれる
渡辺 勝彦 先生 [英語]	「スーパー速読法」で、難解な英文も一発で理解させる超実力講師!
宮崎 尊 先生 [英語]	雑誌『TIME』の翻訳など、英語界でその名を馳せる有名実力講師!
西 きょうじ 先生 [英語]	29年間で20万人以上の受験生に支持されてきた知的刺激溢れる講義をご期待ください。
大岩 秀樹 先生 [英語]	情熱と若さあふれる授業で、知らず知らずのうちに英語が得意教科に!

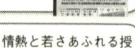

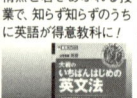

数学

講師	キャッチコピー
志田 晶 先生 [数学]	数学科実力講師は、わかりやすさを徹底的に追求する
長岡 恭史 先生 [数学]	受講者からは理Ⅲを含む東大や国立医学部など超難関大合格者が続出
沖田 一希 先生 [数学]	短期間で数学力を徹底的に養成。知識を統一・体系化する!

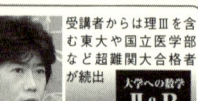

付録 **1**

WEBで体験

東進ドットコムで授業を体験できます！
実力講師陣の詳しい紹介や、各教科の学習アドバイスも読めます。
www.toshin.com/teacher/

国語

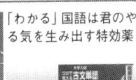

板野 博行 先生 [現代文・古文]
「わかる」国語は君のやる気を生み出す特効薬

出口 汪 先生 [現代文] 
ミスター驚異の現代文。数々のベストセラー著者としても超有名！

吉野 敬介 先生 [古文] 
予備校界の超大物が東進に登場。ドラマチックで熱い講義を体験せよ

富井 健二 先生 [古文] 
ビジュアル解説で古文を簡単明快に解き明かす実力講師

三羽 邦美 先生 [古文・漢文]
縦横無尽な知識に裏打ちされた立体的な授業に、グングン引き込まれる！

樋口 裕一 先生 [小論文]
小論文指導の第一人者。著書「頭がいい人、悪い人の話し方」は250万部突破！

理科

橋元 淳一郎 先生 [物理]
橋元流の解法は君の脳に衝撃を与える！

田部 眞哉 先生 [生物]
全国の受験生が絶賛するその授業は、わかりやすさそのもの！

地歴公民

荒巻 豊志 先生 [世界史]
"受験世界史に荒巻あり"と言われる超実力人気講師

金谷 俊一郎 先生 [日本史] 
入試頻出事項に的を絞った「表解板書」は圧倒的な信頼を得る！

清水 雅博 先生 [公民]
全国の政経受験者が絶賛のベストセラー講師！

合格の秘訣2 革新的な学習システム

東進には、第一志望合格に必要なすべての要素を満たし、抜群の合格実績を生み出す学習システムがあります。

映像による授業を駆使した最先端の勉強法
高速学習

一人ひとりのレベル・目標にぴったりの授業

東進はすべての授業を映像化しています。その数およそ1万種類。これらの授業を個別に受講できるので、一人ひとりのレベル・目標に合った学習が可能です。1.5倍速受講ができるほか自宅のパソコンからも受講できるので、今までにない効率的な学習が実現します。
（一部1.4倍速の授業もあります。）

1年分の授業を最短2週間から1カ月で受講

従来の予備校は、毎週1回の授業。一方、東進の高速学習なら毎日受講することができます。だから、1年分の授業も最短2週間から1カ月程度で修了可能。先取り学習や苦手科目の克服、勉強と部活との両立も実現できます。

現役合格者の声

東京大学 理科Ⅰ類
吉田 樹くん

東進の高速学習なら部活がない時や学校が休みの時にたくさん講座を受講できるので、とても役に立ちました。受験勉強を通じて、早期に勉強を始めることが重要だと強く感じました。

先取りカリキュラム（数学の例）

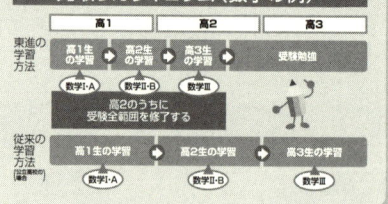

	高1	高2	高3
東進の学習方法	高1生の学習 → 数学Ⅰ・A	高2生の学習 → 数学Ⅱ・B	高3生の学習 → 数学Ⅲ → 受験勉強
	高2のうちに受験全範囲を修了する		
従来の学習方法（一般）	高1生の学習 数学Ⅰ・A	高2生の学習 数学Ⅱ・B	高3生の学習 数学Ⅲ

目標まで一歩ずつ確実に
スモールステップ・パーフェクトマスター

自分にぴったりのレベルから学べる習ったことを確実に身につける

高校入門から超東大までの12段階から自分に合ったレベルを選ぶことが可能です。「簡単すぎる」「難しすぎる」といった無駄がなく、志望校へ最短距離で進みます。授業後すぐにテストを行い内容が身についたかを確認し、合格したら次の授業に進むので、わからない部分を残すことはありません。短期集中で徹底理解をくり返し、学力を高めます。

現役合格者の声

早稲田大学 国際教養学部
竹中 蘭香さん

毎回の授業後にある確認テストと講座の総まとめの講座修了判定テストのおかげで、受講が終わってもほったらかしになりませんでした。授業内容を定着させやすかったです。

パーフェクトマスターのしくみ

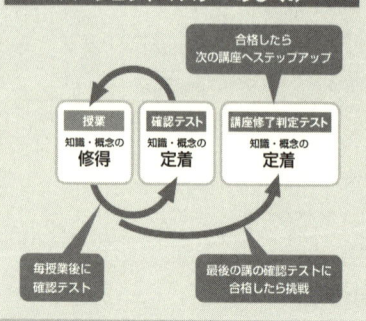

合格したら次の講座へステップアップ

授業 知識・概念の**修得** → **確認テスト** 知識・概念の**定着** → **講座修了判定テスト** 知識・概念の**定着**

毎授業後に確認テスト　　最後の講の確認テストに合格したら挑戦

個別説明会

全国の東進ハイスクール・東進衛星予備校の各校舎にて実施しています。
※お問い合わせ先は、付録9ページをご覧ください。

徹底的に学力の土台を固める

高速基礎マスター講座
（英単語／英熟語／英文法／基本例文）

高速基礎マスター講座は「知識」と「トレーニング」の両面から、科学的かつ効率的に短期間で基礎学力を徹底的に身につけるための講座です。文法事項や重要事項を単元別・分野別にひとつずつ完成させていくことができます。インターネットを介してオンラインで利用できるため、校舎だけでなく、自宅のパソコンやスマートフォンアプリで学習することも可能です。

東進公式スマートフォンアプリ
東進式マスター登場！

スマートフォンアプリですき間時間も徹底活用！

1) スモールステップ・パーフェクトマスター！
頻出度（重要度）の高い英単語から始め、1つのSTEP（計100語）を完全修得すると次のSTAGEに進めるようになります。

2) 自分の英単語力が一目でわかる！
トップ画面に「修得語数・修得率」をメーター表示。自分が今何語修得しているのか、どこを優先的に学習すべきなのか一目でわかります。

3)「覚えていない単語」だけを集中攻略できる！
未修得の単語、または「My単語（自分でチェック登録した単語）」だけをテストする出題設定が可能です。
すでに覚えている単語を何度も学習するような無駄を省き、効率良く単語力を高めることができます。

「新・英単語センター1800」

現役合格者の声

上智大学 理工学部
杉原 里実さん

「高速基礎マスター講座」がおススメです。短い期間で一気に覚えることができるだけでなく、さらにスマートフォンでも学習できるので、とても便利でした。

君を熱誠指導でリードする

担任指導

志望校合格のために君の力を最大限に引き出す

定期的な面談を通じた「熱誠指導」で、生徒一人ひとりのモチベーションを高め、維持するとともに志望校合格までリードする存在、それが東進の「担任」です。

現役合格者の声

慶應義塾大学 法学部
成田 真惟子さん

担任の先生は受験についてのアドバイスだけでなく、将来の夢を見据えて受験することの意味も教えてくださいました。夏期期に辛くなった時には励ましていただき、とても心強かったです。

付録 4

合格の秘訣3 東進ドットコム

ここでしか見られない受験と教育の情報が満載！
大学受験のポータルサイト

www.toshin.com

スマートフォン版も充実！

東進ブックスのインターネット書店
東進WEB書店

ベストセラー参考書から
夢ふくらむ人生の参考書まで

学習参考書から語学・一般書までベストセラー＆ロングセラーの書籍情報がもりだくさん！あなたの「学び」をバックアップするインターネット書店です。検索機能もグンと充実。さらに、一部書籍では立ち読みも可能。探し求める1冊に、きっと出会えます。

付録 5

スマートフォンからもご覧いただけます
東進ドットコムはスマートフォンから簡単アクセス！

最新の入試に対応!!
大学案内

偏差値でも検索できる。検索機能充実！

東進ドットコムの「大学案内」では最新の入試に対応した情報を様々な角度から検索できます。学生の声、入試問題分析、大学校歌など、他では見られない情報が満載！登録は無料です。
また、東進ブックスの『新大学受験案内』では、厳選した185大学を詳しく解説。大学案内とあわせて活用してください。

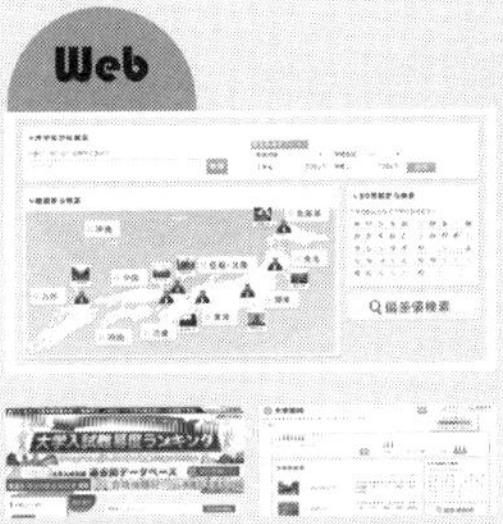

難易度ランキング　50音検索

185大学・最大22年分の過去問を無料で閲覧
大学入試過去問データベース

君が目指す大学の過去問をすばやく検索、じっくり研究！

東進ドットコムの「大学入試問題 過去問データベース」は、志望校の過去問をすばやく検索し、じっくり研究することが可能。185大学の過去問をダウンロードすることができます。センター試験の過去問も最大22年分掲載しています。登録・利用は無料です。志望校対策の「最強の教材」である過去問をフル活用することができます。

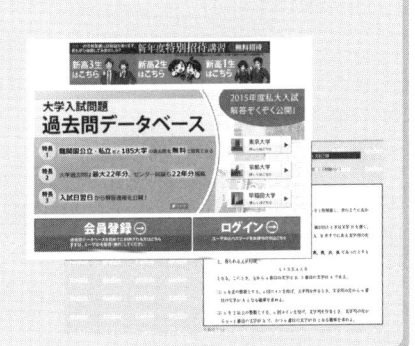

学生特派員からの
先輩レポート

東進OB・OGが生の大学情報をリアルタイムに提供！

東進から難関大学に合格した先輩が、ブログ形式で大学の情報を提供します。大勢の学生特派員によって、学生の目線で伝えられる大学情報が次々とアップデートされていきます。受験を終えたからこそわかるアドバイスも！受験勉強のモチベーションUPに役立つこと間違いなしです。

付録 **6**

合格の秘訣4 東進模試

申込受付中
※お問い合わせ先は付録9ページをご覧ください。

学力を伸ばす模試

「自分の学力を知ること」が受験勉強の第一歩

「絶対評価」×「相対評価」のハイブリッド分析
志望校合格までの距離に加え、受験者集団における順位、および「志望校合否判定」を知ることができます。

入試の『本番レベル』
「合格まであと何点必要か」がわかる。早期に本番レベルを知ることができます。

最短7日のスピード返却
成績表を、最短実施7日後に返却。次の目標に向けた復習はバッチリです。

合格指導解説授業
模試受験後に合格指導解説授業を実施。重要ポイントが手に取るようにわかります。

- 模試受験中に学力を伸ばす！
- 合格までの距離を知り、計画を立てる！
- 学習効果を検証、勉強法を改善する！

全国統一高校生テスト
高3生 高2生 高1生 — 年1回

全国統一中学生テスト
中3生 中2生 中1生 — 年1回

東進模試 ラインアップ 2016年度

模試名	対象	回数
センター試験本番レベル模試	受験生 高2生 高1生 ※高1は難関大志望者	年5回
高校生レベル（マーク・記述）模試	高2生 高1生 ※第1〜3回…マーク、第4回…記述	年4回
東大本番レベル模試	受験生	年3回
京大本番レベル模試	受験生	年3回
北大本番レベル模試	受験生	年2回
東北大本番レベル模試	受験生	年2回
名大本番レベル模試	受験生	年2回
阪大本番レベル模試	受験生	年2回
九大本番レベル模試	受験生	年2回
難関大本番レベル記述模試	受験生	年5回
有名大本番レベル記述模試	受験生	年5回
大学合格基礎力判定テスト	受験生 高2生 高1生	年4回
センター試験同日体験受験	高2生 高1生	年1回
東大入試同日体験受験	高2生 高1生 ※高1は意欲ある東大志望者	年1回

※センター試験本番レベル模試とのドッキング判定

※最終回がセンター試験後の受験となる模試は、センター試験自己採点とのドッキング判定となります。

東進で勉強したいが、近くに校舎がない君は…
東進ハイスクール 在宅受講コースへ

「遠くて東進の校舎に通えない……」。そんな君も大丈夫！ 在宅受講コースなら自宅のパソコンを使って勉強できます。ご希望の方には、在宅受講コースのパンフレットをお送りいたします。お電話にてご連絡ください。学習・進路相談も随時可能です。

2016年も難関大・有名大 ゾクゾク現役合格
日本一※の東大現役合格実績

現役のみ！講習生含みます！

※2015年、東大現役合格実績をホームページ・パンフレット・チラシ等で公表している予備校の中で最大。当社調べ。　2016年3月31日締切

東大現役合格者の2.8人に1人が東進生

東進生現役占有率 36.3%

東大現役合格者 742名（合格者増 +14名）

- 文Ⅰ…125名
- 文Ⅱ…100名
- 文Ⅲ…88名
- 推薦…21名
- 理Ⅰ…247名
- 理Ⅱ…110名
- 理Ⅲ…51名

今年の東大合格者は現浪合わせて3,108名。そのうち、現役合格者は2,043名。東進の現役合格者は742名ですので、東大現役合格者における東進生の占有率は36.3%となります。現役合格者の2.8人に1人が東進生です。合格者の皆さん、おめでとうございます。

現役合格 旧七帝大＋東工大・一橋大 2,980名（合格者増 +194名）

- 東京大……742名
- 京都大……309名
- 北海道大…251名
- 東北大……253名
- 名古屋大…293名
- 大阪大……496名
- 九州大……341名
- 東京工業大…130名
- 一橋大………165名

現役合格 国公立医・医 596名（合格者増 +15名）

東京大	52名	群馬大	11名	大阪市立大	10名
京都大	19名	千葉大	20名	神戸大	11名
北海道大	9名	東京医科歯科大	20名	岡山大	13名
東北大	17名	横浜市立大	10名	広島大	21名
名古屋大	12名	新潟大	10名	徳島大	17名
大阪大	16名	金沢大	16名	香川大	14名
九州大	11名	山梨大	14名	愛媛大	15名
札幌医科大	11名	信州大	8名	佐賀大	17名
弘前大	13名	岐阜大	11名	熊本大	12名
秋田大	11名	浜松医科大	17名	琉球大	11名
福島県立医科大	9名	三重大	11名	その他国公立医・歯	110名
筑波大	16名				

現役合格 早慶 5,071名（合格者増 +173名）

- 早稲田大…3,222名
- 慶應義塾大…1,849名

現役合格 上理明青立法中 16,773名（合格者増 +930名）

- 上智大……1,180名
- 東京理科大…1,937名
- 明治大……3,945名
- 青山学院大…1,680名
- 立教大……2,146名
- 法政大……3,631名
- 中央大……2,254名

現役合格 国公立大 13,762名（合格者増 +714名）

東京工業	130名	東京農工	87名	神戸	374名
一橋	165名	東京海洋	62名	神戸市外国語	57名
北海道教育	69名	横浜国立	281名	兵庫教育	30名
旭川医科	16名	横浜市立	155名	京都女子	51名
北見工業	34名	新潟	212名	京都教育	36名
小樽商科	49名	富山	133名	和歌山	77名
弘前	90名	金沢	198名	鳥取	98名
岩手	57名	福井	69名	島根	78名
宮城	27名	山梨	73名	岡山	265名
秋田	55名	都留文科	65名	広島	293名
国際教養	34名	信州	191名	山口	229名
山形	101名	岐阜	143名	徳島	160名
福島	67名	静岡	225名	香川	105名
筑波	237名	静岡県立	50名	愛媛	204名
茨城	156名	浜松医科	24名	高知	84名
宇都宮	54名	愛知教育	120名	北九州市立	122名
群馬	70名	名古屋工業	150名	九州工業	121名
高崎経済	83名	名古屋市立	128名	福岡教育	67名
埼玉	147名	三重	199名	佐賀	131名
埼玉県立	34名	滋賀	83名	長崎	122名
千葉	335名	滋賀医科	13名	熊本	207名
東京医科歯科	38名	京都教育	29名	大分	78名
東京海洋	112名	京都府立	43名	宮崎	91名
首都大学東京	258名	京都工芸繊維	55名	鹿児島	113名
お茶の水女子	59名	大阪市立	241名	琉球	113名
電気通信	66名	大阪府立	200名		
東京学芸	119名	大阪教育	140名		

※東進調べ

現役合格 関関同立 11,432名（合格者増 +898名）

- 関西学院大…2,273名
- 関西大……2,564名
- 同志社大…2,502名
- 立命館大…4,093名

現役合格 私立医・医 412名 ※防衛医科大学校を含む

- 慶應義塾大…48名
- 順天堂大…43名
- 東京慈恵会医科大…29名
- 昭和大…24名
- 防衛医科大学校…49名
- その他私立医・医 219名

ウェブサイトでもっと詳しく ➡ 東進 🔍 検索

付録 8

各大学の合格実績は、東進ネットワーク（東進ハイスクール・東進衛星予備校・早稲田塾）の合同実績です。

東進へのお問い合わせ・資料請求は
東進ドットコム www.toshin.com
もしくは下記のフリーダイヤルへ！

ハッキリ言って合格実績が自慢です！大学受験なら、
東進ハイスクール　0120-104-555（トーシン ゴーゴーゴー）

●東京都

[中央地区]
- 市ヶ谷校　0120-104-205
- 新宿エルタワー校　0120-104-121
- ※新宿校大学受験本科　0120-104-020
- 高田馬場校　0120-104-770
- 人形町校　0120-104-075

[城北地区]
- 赤羽校　0120-104-293
- 本郷三丁目校　0120-104-068
- 茗荷谷校　0120-738-104

[城東地区]
- 綾瀬校　0120-104-762
- 金町校　0120-452-104
- ★北千住校　0120-693-104
- 錦糸町校　0120-104-249
- 豊洲校　0120-104-282
- 西新井校　0120-266-104
- 西葛西校　0120-289-104
- 門前仲町校　0120-104-016

[城西地区]
- 池袋校　0120-104-062
- 大泉学園校　0120-104-862
- 荻窪校　0120-687-104
- 高円寺校　0120-104-627
- 石神井校　0120-104-159
- 巣鴨校　0120-104-780
- 成増校　0120-028-104
- 練馬校　0120-104-643

[城南地区]
- 大井町校　0120-575-104
- 蒲田校　0120-265-104
- 五反田校　0120-672-104
- 三軒茶屋校　0120-104-739
- 渋谷駅西口校　0120-389-104
- 下北沢校　0120-104-672
- 自由が丘校　0120-964-104
- 成城学園前駅北口校　0120-104-616
- 千歳烏山校　0120-104-331
- 都立大学前校　0120-275-104

[東京都下]
- 吉祥寺校　0120-104-775
- 国立校　0120-104-599
- 国分寺校　0120-622-104
- 立川駅北口校　0120-104-662
- 田無校　0120-104-272
- 調布校　0120-104-305
- 八王子校　0120-896-104
- 東久留米校　0120-565-104
- 府中校　0120-104-676
- ★町田校　0120-104-507
- 武蔵小金井校　0120-480-104
- 武蔵境校　0120-104-769

●神奈川県
- 青葉台校　0120-104-947
- 厚木校　0120-104-716
- 川崎校　0120-226-104
- 湘南台東口校　0120-104-706
- 新百合ヶ丘校　0120-104-182
- センター南駅前校　0120-104-722
- たまプラーザ校　0120-104-445
- 鶴見校　0120-876-104
- 平塚校　0120-104-742
- 藤沢校　0120-104-549
- 向ヶ丘遊園校　0120-104-757
- 武蔵小杉校　0120-165-104
- ★横浜校　0120-104-473

●埼玉県
- 浦和校　0120-104-561
- 大宮校　0120-104-858
- 春日部校　0120-104-508
- 川口校　0120-917-104
- 川越校　0120-104-538
- 小手指校　0120-104-759
- 志木校　0120-104-202
- せんげん台校　0120-104-388
- 草加校　0120-104-690
- 所沢校　0120-104-594
- ★南浦和校　0120-104-573
- 与野校　0120-104-755

●千葉県
- 我孫子校　0120-104-253
- 市川駅前校　0120-104-381
- 稲毛海岸校　0120-104-575
- 海浜幕張校　0120-104-926
- 柏校　0120-104-353
- 北習志野校　0120-344-104
- 新浦安校　0120-556-104
- 新松戸校　0120-104-354
- ★千葉校　0120-104-564
- ★津田沼校　0120-104-724
- 土気校　0120-104-584
- 成田駅前校　0120-104-346
- 船橋校　0120-104-514
- 松戸校　0120-104-257
- 南柏校　0120-104-439
- 八千代台校　0120-104-863

●茨城県
- つくば校　0120-403-104
- 土浦校　0120-059-104
- 取手校　0120-104-328

●静岡県
- 静岡校　0120-104-585

●長野県
- ★長野校　0120-104-586

●奈良県
- JR奈良駅前校　0120-104-746
- 奈良校　0120-104-597

★ = 高卒本科（高卒生）設置校
※ = 高卒生専用校舎

※変更の可能性があります。最新情報はウェブサイトで確認できます。

全国954校、10万人の高校生が通う、
東進衛星予備校　0120-104-531（トーシン ゴーサイン）

東進ドットコムでお近くの校舎を検索！

資料請求もできます

「東進衛星予備校」の「校舎案内」をクリック 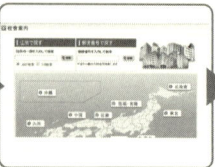　→　エリア・都道府県を選択　→　校舎一覧が確認できます

近くに東進の校舎がない高校生のための
東進ハイスクール 在宅受講コース　0120-531-104（ゴーサイン トーシン）

※2016年3月末現在